The Ultimate Guide For Men With Adult ADHD:

Simple Strategies & Proven Techniques to Improve Focus, Increase Productivity, Manage Symptoms & Thrive in Life

Mark Fitzgerald

<u>Disclaimer</u>

The content of this book is intended for informational and educational purposes only. While we discuss various aspects of life such as relationships, financial management, health, and more, the information provided should not be considered as professional medical, financial, or psychological advice. Always seek the advice of a qualified healthcare provider, financial advisor, or other professional with any questions you may have regarding a medical condition, financial decisions, or other areas of concern. The author and publisher disclaim any liability arising directly or indirectly from the use of this book.

CONTENTS

Introduction

Imagine waking up with a list of tasks on your mind that need to be completed today. John, a 35-year-old graphic designer, wakes up early, determined to tackle his to-do list. His morning starts with a jolt of enthusiasm; he's ready to conquer the world. First, he decides to clean his apartment, which has become increasingly cluttered over the past week. He starts in the living room, picking up a pile of clothes that needs folding.

As he's folding, he notices his laptop on the coffee table and remembers he needs to send an important email to a client. He puts down the clothes and opens his laptop. But before he can compose the email, he notices a new email notification about a sale on his favorite website. He clicks on it, and what was supposed to be a quick glance turns into 20 minutes of online shopping.

Realizing he's strayed from his task, John decides to close his laptop and return to cleaning. But as he's walking back to the living room, he remembers he wanted to text his friend about their weekend plans. He pulls out his phone and, just as he's about to send the text, a social media notification pops up. John taps on it and suddenly finds himself scrolling through his feed, watching videos, and liking posts. Ten minutes later, he puts his phone down and...wait, why did he pick it up in the first place?

John's day continues in this scattered manner. He begins several tasks, each one leading to a distraction that pulls him away from completing anything. By the time evening rolls around, he looks back on his day with frustration. Despite feeling constantly busy, his to-do list remains largely unchecked. The apartment is still a mess, the email remains unsent, and he never did finalize those weekend plans.

This cycle of starting and stopping, of being perpetually busy yet unproductive, is a common experience for men with Adult ADHD. The constant distractions and inability to focus on a single task can leave them feeling overwhelmed and frustrated. Yet, this is not just a series of unfortunate events—it's a glimpse into the daily struggle faced by many with ADHD.

Does John's story sound familiar to you? Or maybe sometimes you find yourself scrambling to keep up with a conversation or feeling overwhelmed by simple daily tasks that others seem to manage effortlessly? If so, you're not alone. Many adult men with ADHD experience these frustrations every day, wrestling with a unique set of challenges that can make ordinary activities feel daunting.

This book is designed to be a guide for you, whether you've been diagnosed with ADHD or suspect you might have it. It's more than just a collection of information; it's a toolkit designed to transform your approach to challenges, enhance your productivity, and improve your overall well-being. I understand these struggles not just professionally but personally, fueling my passion to assist you in navigating the often turbulent waters of adult ADHD.

Through understanding and managing your symptoms, you can learn to harness your unique strengths and lead a more focused, productive and fulfilling life.

My commitment is to offer you a blend of scientifically-backed insights and practical, actionable strategies tailored specifically for adult men. This book combines my years of experience and dedication with motivational elements and a hands-on approach to make a real difference in your life. Each chapter is constructed to build understanding, impart effective strategies, and motivate you to implement what you've learned.

Structured to be engaging and informative, the book includes personal anecdotes that resonate with your daily experiences, the latest research on ADHD, pragmatic advice, and exercises for you to try. Each section addresses different aspects of living with ADHD, from mastering focus and productivity to improving emotional well-being and interpersonal relationships.

As you turn these pages, expect to find not only a source of information but also a source of transformation. This book is intended to be the best guide you've ever read on ADHD, providing a pathway to not just cope with but thrive despite the challenges posed by ADHD.

I invite you to read this book and engage with it actively. Apply the exercises, reflect on the insights, and embrace the journey of improvement. It's time to shift your perspective on ADHD and see it not as a barrier but as a unique aspect of who you are, capable of being shaped into a strength.

Let's begin this journey together, with hope and a clear action plan, towards a more focused and fulfilling life.

Just before we dive right into the chapters here are some typical symptoms of adult ADHD in men.

Symptoms of Adult ADHD in Men

Adult ADHD manifests in various ways, and its symptoms can significantly impact daily life. Understanding these symptoms and their examples can help men recognize and manage their ADHD more effectively. Here are some common symptoms and practical examples:

1. Inattention

Men with ADHD often struggle with maintaining focus, especially on tasks that are not inherently interesting to them. This can manifest as:

- **Example:** During meetings, a man might find his mind wandering, missing key points of the discussion. At home, he might start a project like fixing a leaky faucet but get distracted halfway through by a notification on his phone, leaving the task incomplete.

2. Hyperactivity

While hyperactivity tends to be more pronounced in children, adults with ADHD can still exhibit signs of restlessness and an inability to stay still.

- **Example:** A man might feel the need to constantly fidget or tap his foot during work hours. He may also prefer to take on physically demanding tasks or engage in frequent movement, such as pacing while on the phone.

3. Impulsivity

Impulsivity can lead to hasty decisions without considering the consequences, often leading to social, financial, and professional issues.

- **Example:** In a social setting, he might interrupt others frequently or blurt out thoughts without filtering them. Financially, he might make spontaneous purchases that he later regrets, such as buying an expensive gadget without budgeting for it.

4. Disorganization

Men with ADHD often struggle with organizing tasks, managing time, and maintaining orderly spaces.

- **Example:** His workspace might be cluttered with papers, books, and office supplies, making it hard to find important documents. He might also miss deadlines or arrive late to appointments because of poor time management.

5. Poor Time Management

Difficulty in perceiving time accurately can result in chronic lateness or rushed, last-minute efforts.

- **Example:** He might underestimate how long a task will take, leading to being consistently late for meetings. Alternatively, he might procrastinate on starting a project until the last minute, resulting in a hurried, subpar completion.

6. Forgetfulness

Forgetfulness can affect daily responsibilities and obligations, causing stress and frustration.

- **Example:** He might forget to pay bills on time, leading to late fees. He might also frequently lose personal items like keys, glasses, or his wallet, disrupting his routine.

7. Emotional Dysregulation

Men with ADHD might experience intense emotional responses and difficulty regulating their emotions.

- **Example:** He might have sudden outbursts of anger over minor frustrations, like a traffic jam. Conversely, he might feel overwhelmed by tasks that seem manageable to others, leading to feelings of inadequacy and anxiety.

8. Difficulty Prioritizing Tasks

Struggling to determine which tasks are most important can lead to inefficiency and stress.

- **Example:** He might spend a significant amount of time on low-priority tasks, such as organizing his email inbox, while neglecting critical projects with looming deadlines.

9. Procrastination

Procrastination is common, often resulting from a fear of failure or feeling overwhelmed by the task at hand.

- **Example:** He might delay starting a major report until the night before it's due, resulting in high stress and a lower quality of work than he is capable of producing.

10. Relationship Issues

ADHD symptoms can strain relationships with family, friends, and colleagues due to misunderstandings and unmet expectations.

- **Example:** He might forget important dates like anniversaries or fail to follow through on commitments, causing frustration and disappointment in his partner. In professional settings, he might miss deadlines or fail to complete tasks, leading to tension with coworkers and supervisors.

Chapter 1: The ADHD Brain Demystified

Have you ever stopped to wonder why your brain seems to operate differently from others? While everyone else seems to follow a straight path, your mind takes a scenic route, filled with unexpected stops and starts. This isn't just a quirk of your personality; it's deeply rooted in the neurology of a brain with ADHD. Understanding the architecture of your brain and its unique chemistry can be like finding a map that explains previously confusing journeys. This chapter will guide you through the inner workings of the ADHD brain, focusing specifically on the critical roles played by the prefrontal cortex, executive functions, and the delicate balance of neurotransmitters that influence your everyday life.

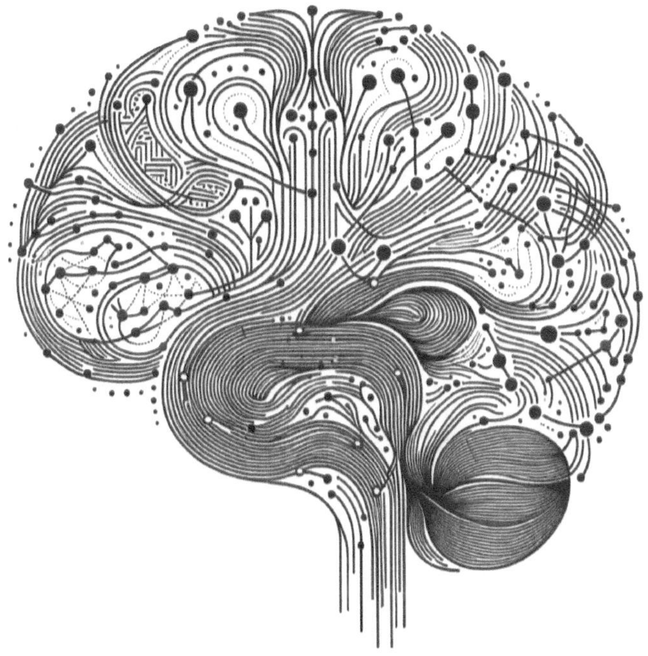

The Neurology of ADHD: Unpacking the Executive Functions

The Role of the Prefrontal Cortex

The prefrontal cortex is like the CEO of your brain—it's responsible for high-level functions such as decision making, problem-solving, and regulating social behavior. In adult men with ADHD, this area of the brain can behave somewhat unpredictably. Typically, the pre-frontal cortex helps manage what we call executive functions: these are the command systems of our brains, overseeing tasks like organizing, planning, and prioritizing. However, when you have ADHD, your prefrontal cortex may not perform these duties consistently. This inconsistency can lead to difficulties in maintaining attention, managing emotions, and executing tasks efficiently.

Research suggests that this part of the brain in individuals with ADHD is often underactive, leading to less inhibition and poorer organizational skills. This underactivity can make it challenging to filter distractions, leading to the common symptoms of inattentiveness and impulsivity seen in many adults with ADHD. Understanding this aspect of brain function is crucial because it highlights that ADHD isn't a flaw in character but rather a neurological condition that requires specific strategies to manage.

Understanding Executive Dysfunction

Executive dysfunction is a hallmark of ADHD and can manifest in various ways, significantly impacting your daily life. For example, you might find it hard to start a project, organize your tasks, or follow through with plans. This isn't due to a lack of effort or motivation but rather a part of how your brain operates. The executive functions, governed mainly by your prefrontal cortex, are what allow individuals to plan for the future, evaluate the outcomes of their actions, and suppress inappropriate behaviors. When these functions are disrupted, it can feel as if your brain's command center is misfiring.

Practically, this means that tasks requiring sequential steps can become overwhelming. Organizing your workspace, managing your time, and even keeping up with social obligations can become Herculean tasks. Many men with ADHD describe the frustration of knowing what they need to do but finding it nearly impossible to execute these plans in an organized manner.

Neurotransmitter Dynamics

Dopamine and norepinephrine are two critical neurotransmitters in the brain that are particularly relevant to ADHD. These chemicals help transmit signals in your brain and play significant roles in regulating mood, sleep, attention, and learning. In the ADHD brain, there are often imbalances in these neurotransmitters, which can affect how you concentrate and manage emotions.

Dopamine, often dubbed the "feel-good" neurotransmitter, is linked to the reward center of your brain. For someone with ADHD, lower levels of dopamine can make it hard to stay motivated or derive pleasure from activities that others might find rewarding. Norepinephrine affects how you respond to stress and how you concentrate on tasks. An imbalance here can mean that you either overreact or are too stressed, or you find it difficult to focus your attention when necessary.

Understanding these dynamics is not just about pinpointing deficits; it's about identifying ways to balance these chemicals, possibly through medication, diet, exercise, or other therapies. Tailoring treatments to your specific neurotransmitter needs can significantly improve your quality of life and functionality.

ADHD Diagnosis and the Brain

Diagnosing ADHD is more than just identifying behaviors; it involves a comprehensive evaluation that may include brain scans like MRI or CT scans to rule out other neurological conditions. These imaging techniques can sometimes show patterns consistent with ADHD, such as reduced activity in the prefrontal cortex. However, a diagnosis primarily relies on clinical evaluations, including psychological questionnaires, behavioral assessments, and sometimes, physical exams.

The process is thorough because it's crucial to differentiate ADHD from other possible disorders and to understand how extensively ADHD affects you. This comprehensive approach ensures that the treatment plan is as effective and personalized as possible, addressing your unique brain chemistry and life circumstances.

Understanding the neurological underpinnings of ADHD is the first step in demystifying the condition and moving towards effective management strategies. By comprehending how your brain is structured and operates, you can better navigate the challenges and utilize your strengths more effectively. This knowledge empowers you to make informed decisions about treatments and adjustments in your daily life, leading to improved outcomes and a more satisfying life trajectory.

Hyperfocus vs. Distraction: The ADHD Paradox

Defining Hyperfocus

Hyperfocus can be a double-edged sword for many men with ADHD. It is a state where one becomes completely absorbed in a task that interests them, to the exclusion of all other external stimuli. This intense concentration can lead you to produce high-quality work and innovative solutions to complex problems, often in a surprisingly short amount of time. However, the challenge arises when this hyperfocus diverts attention from crucial tasks that might not be as engaging but are equally necessary.

Picture this: You're working on a graphic design project, and the creative juices are flowing. Hours slip by unnoticed because you are wrapped up in perfecting every detail of the design. While this can lead to a stellar final product, you might simultaneously neglect important calls, skip meals, or even forget other critical deadlines. Thus, while hyperfocus can lead you to remarkable achievements in areas of great interest, it can also lead to significant disruptions in both personal and professional life. Understanding when and why hyperfocus kicks in is crucial. Typically, it emerges when engaging in activities that naturally pique your curiosity or challenge your skills—tasks that stimulate dopamine production in your brain, a neurotransmitter often running low in the ADHD brain.

The Mechanics of Distraction

On the flip side of hyperfocus is the ever-present potential for distraction, a common hallmark for men with ADHD. Distraction occurs when your brain is seeking stimulation that the current task may not provide. This search for a dopamine boost can result in difficulties in maintaining focus on tasks that are repetitive, uninteresting, or particularly challenging. The role of external stimuli is significant here; a noisy office, the buzz of your phone, or even the activity outside your window can easily pull your attention away from the task at hand.

This susceptibility to distraction isn't merely about a lack of willpower or discipline; it's deeply rooted in the ADHD brain's neurology. The underactivity in the prefrontal cortex, as discussed earlier, affects your ability to ignore irrelevant stimuli. Thus, your brain's filtering system doesn't work as efficiently as it might in someone without ADHD, making it harder to stay on task. This scenario is further complicated by the inconsistent regulation of neurotransmitters like dopamine and norepinephrine, which are crucial for focus and attention regulation.

Balancing Hyperfocus and Distraction

Managing the delicate balance between hyperfocus and distraction is key to harnessing the full potential of your ADHD. One effective strategy is the use of structured breaks. For instance, employing the Pomodoro Technique—working for focused intervals, typically 25 minutes, followed by a five-minute break—can help manage energy and attention. This method not only curbs the propensity for hyperfocus by setting a clear endpoint but also structures your time in a way that can enhance focus and reduce the likelihood of distraction. We will dive a little deeper into the Pomodoro Technique in the coming chapters.

Another strategy involves creating an environment conducive to focus. This might mean using noise-canceling headphones to block out distracting sounds or organizing your workspace to minimize clutter and visual distractions. Additionally, prioritizing tasks each day and setting clear goals can help keep your brain engaged in the activities that matter most, rather than those that simply feel most urgent or interesting at the moment.

Utilizing Hyperfocus Effectively

When channeled correctly, hyperfocus is an incredible asset. To make the most of this ability, it's crucial to align your periods of potential hyperfocus with your most critical or challenging tasks. This might involve scheduling demanding creative work or complex problem-solving tasks during times when you're typically at your best, mentally and physically.

Furthermore, being mindful of what triggers your hyperfocus can allow you to engineer these triggers into your day-to-day activities to foster productivity. For example, if engaging in a particular type of analytical work tends to draw you in, save this work for periods when you anticipate distractions or when you typically struggle with focus. This proactive approach turns a natural inclination of your ADHD into a powerful tool for accomplishing both routine and complex tasks.

By understanding and managing these aspects of ADHD, you can transform what might often seem like significant hurdles into powerful tools for success. The key lies in not just working harder, but working smarter by leveraging the natural tendencies of your neurodiverse brain to your advantage.

Emotional Dysregulation: Beyond the Stereotypes

Emotions play a complex role in the lives of all human beings, but for men with ADHD, the emotional landscape can often feel particularly intense and uncontrollable. This phenomenon, deeply rooted in the neurobiology of ADHD, is not just about experiencing emotions; it's about how these emotions are processed and regulated by the brain. The neurological underpinnings that link ADHD to heightened emotional responses are primarily found in the way the brain's regulatory systems interact with neural pathways that govern emotions.

In individuals with ADHD, the emotional dysregulation often observed can be tied back to an underactive prefrontal cortex, the brain region responsible for managing executive functions, which includes emotion regulation. When this area is not functioning optimally, it struggles to moderate responses to emotional stimuli, leading to what can be perceived as overreactions to relatively minor events. For example, a mildly critical comment from a colleague might trigger an disproportionately intense feeling of rejection or anger. This heightened emotional sensitivity not only affects interpersonal interactions but can also lead to a rollercoaster of emotions that impact self-esteem and overall mental well-being.

The impact of emotional dysregulation is pervasive and multifaceted. In personal relationships, it can create a minefield of misunderstandings and conflicts. Partners and friends may find the intense or unpredictable emotional reactions perplexing or difficult to cope with, potentially leading to strained relationships. Professionally, emotional dysregulation can manifest as overreacting to feedback, struggling to handle stress, or fluctuating motivation, which can hinder job performance and satisfaction. On a personal level, the constant emotional turbulence can erode self-esteem, as individuals feel unable to control their reactions and become increasingly self-critical about their inability to 'keep their emotions in check.'

Managing these intense emotional responses requires a multi-pronged approach. One effective technique is mindfulness, which involves a focused awareness on the present moment while calmly acknowledging and accepting one's feelings, thoughts, and bodily sensations. Regular mindfulness practice can enhance emotional regulation by improving the ability to observe and identify emotions without immediate reaction, creating a space between feeling and action. Cognitive-behavioral strategies also play a crucial role; these techniques help reframe irrational thoughts that often amplify emotional reactions. By challenging these automatic negative thoughts, individuals can develop more balanced and less distressing responses to emotional triggers.

Another layer of the emotional challenges often faced by men with ADHD is Rejection Sensitive Dysphoria (RSD), a condition where individuals experience intense discomfort, anxiety, or anger in response to perceived or real rejection or criticism. RSD can be debilitating, leading to avoidance of social situations, exaggerated fears of failure, and even rapid shifts in mood. Understanding RSD's role in emotional dysregulation in ADHD is crucial because it highlights the need for targeted strategies that address these intense sensitivity issues. Coping strategies for RSD include therapy techniques that focus on building resilience to criticism and rejection, such as cognitive-behavioral therapy (CBT) and dialectical behavior therapy (DBT). These therapies provide tools for managing the intense emotions associated with RSD and can help individuals reinterpret their emotional responses to rejection in a healthier, more balanced way.

In essence, navigating the complexities of emotional dysregulation when you have ADHD involves understanding the neurological basis of your emotional processes, recognizing the profound impact these can have on your daily life, and actively employing strategies to manage and mitigate these effects. By doing so, you can begin to take control of your emotional responses, improve your interactions with others, and enhance your self-esteem and personal well-being. This understanding and approach are not just about managing symptoms but are about transforming potentially debilitating sensitivity into a pathway for emotional growth and resilience.

Time Perception and ADHD: Why "Just a Minute" Feels Different

Understanding Time Blindness

Time blindness is a term that might sound unfamiliar, yet it encapsulates a daily reality for many men with ADHD. It refers to the difficulty in understanding and managing the passage of time. This isn't just about being a few minutes late or misjudging the length of a meeting; it's about a fundamental disconnect between your perception of time and its actual progression. Imagine you're engrossed in work, perhaps it's a project you find particularly engaging, and you believe only a short period has passed. Upon checking the time, you're shocked to find out several hours have flown by. This distortion isn't a rare mishap; it's a frequent occurrence that can lead to a cascade of personal and professional challenges.

For someone without ADHD, time might seem to flow in a steady, predictable stream — each minute following the last at the same interval, each hour marked by a consistent rhythm. For someone with ADHD, however, time can feel like a river after a storm, ebbing and flowing unpredictably, with calm stretches suddenly accelerating into rapids. This irregular perception can make it extraordinarily difficult to navigate a world that operates on strict schedules and deadlines. You might find yourself either massively overestimating or underestimating how much time you have to complete tasks, leading to last-minute rushes or missed opportunities.

The Impact on Daily Life

The practical implications of time blindness are far-reaching. Consider punctuality, a basic societal expectation. If you consistently misjudge the time it takes to get ready or travel somewhere, you're often seen as unreliable or disrespectful, which can strain professional relationships and personal connections alike. Then there's procrastination — not always a result of laziness or lack of motivation as often misunderstood. For you, it might stem from an inaccurate sense of how much time tasks actually take. A project you estimate will take two hours might realistically require five, but by the time this becomes apparent, deadlines might be looming dangerously close.

Effective time management is often predicated on the ability to anticipate future needs and schedule accordingly. However, if your perception of time is skewed, planning becomes a daunting task. It's like trying to navigate with a compass that doesn't point north. The frustration that arises from repeatedly feeling out of sync can lead to a cycle of stress and decreased productivity, which only serves to exacerbate the sense of being overwhelmed and behind on your responsibilities.

Neurological Basis for Time Perception Issues

The roots of time blindness in ADHD can be traced back to neurological differences. The prefrontal cortex, which we've discussed as the executive center of the brain, plays a crucial role in time perception and management. In ADHD, the reduced activity in this region affects your ability to gauge the passage of time accurately. Moreover, the neurotransmitters dopamine and norepinephrine, which are in flux in the ADHD brain, contribute significantly to how you perceive and value time. Dopamine has a hand in reward processing and motivation, which can affect how you prioritize tasks and perceive their duration. Norepinephrine affects alertness and arousal, influencing how you pay attention to and process the concept of time.

Scientific studies have shown that these neurotransmitter imbalances and cortical under-activations lead to difficulties in something called 'time estimation' — the ability to gauge how long something will take or how much time has passed. This isn't just about looking at a clock and understanding the hour; it's about an internal sense of time, which for many with ADHD, can often seem to be out of tune.

Tools and Strategies for Improving Time Management

Addressing time perception difficulties involves a mixture of external tools and internal adjustments. One effective approach is the use of highly visible clocks and timers. Digital timers can be set to remind you of how much time has passed, or how much is left, helping to anchor your perception of time to something concrete. Alarms and alerts can also be set on smartphones or smartwatches, serving as external cues to keep you aligned with real-world time demands.

Another strategy involves the breaking down of tasks into smaller, more manageable segments. This method, known as "time chunking," allows for a more accurate estimation of how long activities will actually take. Each segment becomes a mini-deadline, providing regular check-ins on your progress and helping recalibrate your sense of time if you begin to drift. Additionally, visual schedules can play a significant role. These might include color-coded calendars or planning apps that help you visualize how your time is allocated throughout the day or week, making it easier to understand and manage at a glance.

Employing these tools and strategies doesn't just help mitigate the challenges of time blindness; it enables you to take control of your time, rather than feeling constantly chased or surprised by it. By developing a toolkit that addresses your unique perception of time, you can enhance your productivity, meet obligations with less stress, and improve your overall quality of life.

Rejection Sensitive Dysphoria: The Hidden Emotional Depth of ADHD

Defining RSD

Rejection Sensitive Dysphoria (RSD) manifests as an extreme emotional sensitivity and pain triggered by the perception that one has been rejected or criticized by important people in their life. Unlike typical emotional responses where feelings of disappointment or sadness might be proportional and fleeting, RSD experiences are intense, overwhelming, and often disproportionate. These feelings can strike suddenly and can feel almost like physical pain. It is as if the emotional response dial has been turned up, where even constructive criticism or a mild rebuke can evoke a profound reaction, akin to a severe emotional wound.

What differentiates RSD from more common types of sensitivity is its profound intensity and the significant impairment it can impose on a person's life. This isn't just about feeling unusually bad about a negative comment or a disapproving look; it's about experiencing these incidents as catastrophic, and they can lead to an immediate and all-encompassing shutdown of emotional composure. For men with ADHD, who are often already grappling with emotional regulation issues, RSD can add an additional layer of complexity to their daily social interactions and internal emotional stability.

The ADHD Connection

Exploring why RSD is particularly prevalent among men with ADHD requires delving into the nuances of the ADHD brain. Research indicates that ADHD is not just about attention challenges but also involves significant difficulties with emotional regulation. The brain regions involved in controlling emotions, particularly the limbic system and the frontal cortex, do not communicate as effectively in individuals with ADHD. This lack of coordination can make it hard for them to moderate their emotional responses.

Moreover, the neurotransmitter differences that characterize ADHD, especially involving dopamine which is crucial for emotional regulation, further complicate this dynamic. Dopamine dysregulation not only affects attention and focus but also plays a critical role in emotional wellbeing. This imbalance can make individuals with ADHD more prone to mood swings and emotional impulsivity, key contributors to the development of RSD. Additionally, many individuals with ADHD have faced a history of real or perceived rejections and criticisms from early childhood due to their symptoms, which can sensitize them to future interactions, priming their emotional responses to be more intense.

RSD's Impact on Self-Esteem and Relationships

The implications of RSD on self-esteem and relationships can be profound. The intense emotional pain caused by perceived rejection can lead to avoidance of social situations, reluctance to form new relationships, or a hypersensitivity that puts a strain on existing relationships. In romantic relationships, misunderstandings and conflicts can escalate quickly because the emotional stakes seem so high and reactions can be swift and severe. Professionally, feedback, which is often a routine part of any job, can become a trigger for emotional turmoil, leading to job dissatisfaction and a constant fear of evaluation.

On a personal level, the repeated impact of RSD can erode self-esteem. Each perceived rejection reinforces negative self-perceptions, potentially trapping individuals in a cycle of self-doubt and depression. They might start to view themselves as fundamentally unlikable or incapable, beliefs that can be deeply internalized and difficult to shake. This ongoing battle can make everyday interactions feel fraught with potential emotional landmines, making it challenging to navigate the simplest social landscapes.

Coping Mechanisms and Solutions

Addressing RSD effectively involves a combination of recognition, therapeutic strategies, and sometimes, medication. Recognizing the signs of RSD is the first critical step—acknowledging that this is not merely an overreaction, but a distinct and extreme emotional response to perceived criticism or rejection. Education about RSD can also help individuals and their loved ones understand the nature of these reactions, fostering empathy and better communication.

Therapeutic strategies, particularly cognitive-behavioral therapy (CBT), can be effective in helping to manage RSD. CBT focuses on changing negative thought patterns and behaviors, which can be particularly beneficial in addressing the distorted thinking associated with RSD. Techniques such as cognitive restructuring can help individuals reframe their perceptions of social interactions and reduce the intensity of their emotional responses. Mindfulness and stress reduction techniques can also assist in managing the physiological reactions to emotional triggers.

In some cases, medication may be a helpful component of treatment, especially if RSD symptoms are significantly impairing or if they exist alongside other psychiatric conditions such as major depressive disorder or anxiety disorders. Medications that help regulate dopamine and norepinephrine levels might not only improve focus and attention in ADHD but also help stabilize mood swings and reduce the sensitivity to rejection.

Implementing these coping mechanisms requires patience and persistence. It involves a continuous process of learning and adapting strategies that best fit the individual's unique circumstances and needs. Over time, with consistent effort and support, individuals can develop a more robust emotional framework that allows them to experience social interactions and criticism without the intense pain previously associated with RSD. This transformative process is not about suppressing sensitivity but about building resilience and understanding, turning what once felt like overwhelming obstacles into manageable emotional landscapes.

CHAPTER 2: ADHD AND IDENTITY

I magine standing at a crossroads where every path is labeled with a different aspect of your identity. One sign points to "Professional," another to "Partner," or "Friend," and yet another, prominently, to "ADHD." It's easy to feel that this last sign is more defining than the others, casting a long shadow over your self-perception and how others see you. Yet, what if you could see this sign not as a roadblock but as a unique marker guiding you toward untapped strengths and potential? This chapter delves into reframing ADHD from a label that confines to a trait that empowers, exploring its place within the concept of neurodiversity, challenging the stigma, and celebrating the unique strengths it can bestow.

Beyond the Label: Reframing ADHD as a Neurodiverse Strength

ADHD as Part of Neurodiversity

Neurodiversity is a perspective that brain differences are just that: differences, not deficits. It encompasses a range of conditions like Autism Spectrum Disorder, Dyslexia, and yes, ADHD. Each of these conditions can contribute to the human mosaic with their unique sets of challenges and strengths. Understanding ADHD within this context can radically change how you perceive yourself and how you navigate your challenges. It encourages the view that your brain's wiring, characterized by ADHD, offers a distinct way of thinking and interacting with the world—a perspective that can lead to innovative problem-solving, hyperfocused creativity, and heightened empathy towards others' struggles. When you start to see ADHD as a different ability rather than a disability, the narrative shifts from one of limitation to one of potential.

Challenging the Stigma

Despite growing awareness, the stigma surrounding ADHD persists, often fuelled by misconceptions and misinformation. Society frequently paints ADHD as a disorder of childhood, marked by hyperactivity and disciplinary problems, ignoring the broad spectrum of how it manifests in adults. This stigma can lead to feelings of shame and inadequacy, making it difficult to seek help or share experiences. Challenging this stigma begins with conversation and education. Sharing your experiences, both the struggles and the triumphs, can help demystify the condition. It's about showing that having ADHD doesn't mean you lack discipline or intelligence but that you interact with the world in a way that others might not immediately understand. By engaging in open dialogues, whether in personal circles or public platforms, you help break down the barriers of misunderstanding and pave the way for a more accepting society.

Identifying Unique Strengths

Living with ADHD can often feel like an uphill battle. However, many of those with ADHD possess a host of unique strengths that can sometimes be overshadowed by their challenges. For instance, your ability to hyperfocus can lead to exceptional productivity and innovation in areas you are passionate about. Your tendency to think outside conventional frameworks can result in creative solutions to complex problems. Moreover, many individuals with ADHD exhibit remarkable resilience—the result of navigating daily challenges that others may take for granted. Identifying and embracing these strengths is not just about building self-esteem; it's about redefining your capabilities and understanding how they can be directed in fulfilling and productive ways.

Success Stories

Consider the stories of those who have turned their ADHD into a superpower. A well-known example is Sir Richard Branson, the dyslexic billionaire entrepreneur who credits his success in part to his ADHD traits of creativity and risk-taking. There's also Simone Biles, who has spoken openly about her ADHD diagnosis and has not let it define her limits but rather her strengths, pushing her to become one of the most decorated gymnasts in history. These stories are not just anecdotes; they are powerful reminders of what is possible when you leverage the unique aspects of your ADHD. They serve as inspiration to look beyond the difficulties and to envision a path where ADHD traits are not just managed but are actively harnessed to achieve success and fulfillment.

In this light, ADHD is not just a challenge to be managed but a different perspective to be understood and valued. It's about shifting the narrative from one of deficit to one of difference, recognizing the unique contributions that your neurodiverse brain can make to society. By reframing ADHD in this way, you not only begin to see yourself in a new light but also invite others to recognize and appreciate the diversity of human cognition.

The Myth of the ADHD Personality: Understanding Individual Variability

When discussing ADHD, it's crucial to sweep aside the one-size-fits-all narrative often portrayed in popular media and even in casual conversations. The depiction of individuals with ADHD as invariably impulsive, perpetually disorganized, or endlessly energetic does a disservice to the rich diversity of personalities and experiences within this community. Such stereotypes not only simplify what is a complex condition but also risk overshadowing the myriad ways in which ADHD manifests from person to person.

Consider for a moment the vast range of personalities and talents among those without ADHD; the same variety applies to those with it. ADHD does not dictate personality; it influences certain traits that might affect how personality is expressed. For instance, while one individual might channel their hyperactivity into a dynamic, go-getter attitude in entrepreneurial ventures, another might experience it as inner restlessness, making reflective, creative pursuits more challenging yet deeply rewarding. Some might find that their impulsivity leads to a charming spontaneity in social situations, while for others, it might require careful management to navigate professional settings successfully. This variability underscores the importance of viewing ADHD symptoms as just one component of a person's overall character and behavioral makeup.

The conflation of personality traits with ADHD symptoms can lead to misunderstandings about the nature of the disorder and about those who live with it. It's essential to distinguish between what behaviors are symptomatic of ADHD and what are inherent personality traits. For example, a person might have a naturally buoyant, outgoing personality, which is not a symptom of ADHD, though their tendency to jump quickly from one topic to another in conversations might be. Similarly, a reflective, introverted individual might still experience impulsivity or emotional dysregulation, which are symptoms not typically associated with such a personality type. Recognizing this distinction helps in accurately understanding and managing ADHD, allowing individuals and those around them to better differentiate between what is a manageable symptom and what is a fundamental aspect of their personality.

Moreover, the environment plays a pivotal role in how ADHD symptoms are expressed and managed. In a supportive, understanding environment, an individual with ADHD might thrive, finding innovative ways to channel their unique traits into productive and fulfilling endeavors. Conversely, in settings that are rigid, overly structured, or critical of their intrinsic way of being, the same individual might struggle significantly. Environments that recognize and adapt to the needs of those with ADHD can transform the expression of ADHD traits from potential hindrances to assets. For instance, workplaces that allow for flexible scheduling might find that employees with ADHD not only perform better but also bring a level of creativity and problem-solving abilities that is highly beneficial.

Embracing individuality, irrespective of an ADHD diagnosis, is a powerful step toward self-acceptance and confidence. It involves recognizing and valuing the unique blend of traits each person brings, rather than defining oneself or others solely by the presence of ADHD. This embrace of individuality encourages a richer, more nuanced understanding of oneself and fosters a greater appreciation for the diversity within the ADHD community and beyond. It challenges each person to find and cultivate their strengths and to approach their challenges with a sense of ownership and creativity, rather than resignation. In doing so, it not only enhances personal growth and satisfaction but also enriches the relationships and communities of which they are a part.

By debunking stereotypes and promoting a more personalized understanding of ADHD, we open the door to more nuanced support systems, better self-awareness, and more fulfilling lives for those with ADHD. It's about moving beyond labels to a deeper understanding of the individual, their environment, and the interplay between the two. This shift in perspective is not just beneficial for those with ADHD; it enriches our broader societal understanding of diversity and the many forms that human attributes can take.

Cultivating Self-Compassion: Strategies for Overcoming Internalized Stigma

When you live with ADHD, the world doesn't always see you the way you see yourself. Sometimes it reflects a distorted image, shaped by misunderstandings and prejudices about what ADHD means. This reflection can be internalized, subtly coloring your self-perception and eroding your self-esteem. This internalized stigma isn't just about absorbing negative views from society; it's about how these views become intertwined with your identity, often making you your own harshest critic. Recognizing and addressing this internalized stigma is crucial, not only for your mental health but for embracing your full potential without the shadow of societal biases.

Internalized stigma manifests in various ways—perhaps it's the belief that you're inherently less capable of success due to your ADHD, or that you must work harder than others just to be seen as competent.

It can lead to a relentless drive for perfection, setting impossibly high standards for yourself, or to a withdrawal from challenges for fear of confirming these negative stereotypes. The danger here is significant: it doesn't just limit your opportunities; it dampens your spirit and your willingness to pursue your passions. Breaking free from this cycle starts with understanding its origins and actively cultivating self-compassion.

Self-compassion involves treating yourself with the same kindness and understanding that you would offer a good friend. It's acknowledging that everyone has challenges and setbacks, and that having ADHD doesn't make you less worthy of happiness or success. This mindset is particularly vital in the face of ADHD, where everyday tasks can sometimes feel like battles. By fostering self-compassion, you start shifting the internal narrative from one of criticism and self-doubt to one of encouragement and resilience.

Practical exercises can be instrumental in building this self-compassion. Mindfulness, for instance, plays a pivotal role. It's about being present in the moment and observing your thoughts and feelings without judgment. Start with simple breathing exercises; focus on your breath, and notice the thoughts that come and go. If you find yourself spiraling into self-criticism, gently acknowledge the thought, then let it pass, bringing your focus back to your breath. This practice can help you gain critical distance from negative thoughts, viewing them as just thoughts, not truths. We will dive a lot deeper into more mindfulness practices in future chapters.

Journaling is another powerful tool. It can provide clarity by allowing you to express thoughts and emotions that might be too complex to untangle in your head. Try writing letters to yourself during different life phases—perhaps writing to your younger self about the challenges you've faced, or to your future self about the hopes you hold. This exercise not only fosters a sense of compassion towards your own journey but also reinforces the understanding that your path is unique and valuable, irrespective of the hurdles.

Building a supportive community is equally important in this journey towards self-compassion. Surround yourself with people who understand and appreciate the complexities of ADHD, whether they are friends, family members, or peers in support groups. These communities can offer not just empathy and encouragement but also practical strategies for dealing with similar challenges. They serve as a reminder that you're not alone in this, that your struggles are understood and shared by many others, and that together, resilience can be built.

Professionally guided support can also be crucial. Therapists, especially those experienced with ADHD, can provide personalized strategies to combat internalized stigma and build self-compassion. They can help you navigate the intricacies of your thoughts and emotions, offering tools that are tailored to your specific needs and circumstances. These professionals can act as guides, helping you to reconstruct a self-image that's based on your strengths and potential rather than misconceptions and stigma.

In cultivating self-compassion, you're not just learning to be kinder to yourself; you're also undoing the knots of internalized stigma that might have held you back. It's about recognizing your worth and your strengths, understanding your challenges, and approaching them with kindness and patience. This transformation in how you view yourself can open up new avenues for growth, happiness, and success, grounded not in societal approval but in genuine self-acceptance.

ADHD Myths vs. Reality: Debunking Common Misconceptions

In a world brimming with information, distinguishing fact from fiction can sometimes feel like navigating a labyrinth. Particularly with ADHD, myths and misconceptions abound, shaping how society perceives and how you might view your own condition. It's crucial, then, to clear the fog around these myths with the bright light of truth, ensuring that both you and those around you have a clear, accurate understanding of what ADHD entails.

One pervasive myth is that ADHD is a childhood condition, suggesting that individuals outgrow it as they mature into adults. This myth fails to recognize that ADHD is a lifelong neurological condition. While symptoms might evolve—the hyperactivity of a child might morph into restlessness in an adult—the core challenges remain. Another common misconception is that ADHD is the result of poor parenting or a lack of discipline. This stigma can be particularly damaging, casting undue blame on families and overshadowing the biological and neurological underpinnings of ADHD. It's essential to understand that ADHD has a strong genetic component and is linked to brain structure and function, not parenting styles.

Additionally, there's a misconception that ADHD is just about lacking focus, ignoring the nuance that those with ADHD often experience what's known as hyperfocus, a state of being deeply engrossed in tasks that are stimulating and rewarding. This aspect can sometimes lead to significant achievements in specific areas, contrary to the stereotype of constant distractibility. By debunking these myths, we pave the way for a more nuanced understanding and approach to managing ADHD, fostering environments that support rather than stigmatize.

Grounding our understanding in scientific facts is the next logical step in dispelling myths. Research shows that ADHD involves multiple neurotransmitters, not just dopamine but also norepinephrine, which plays a crucial role in regulating attention and response inhibition. Imaging studies have illustrated differences in the structure and function of the brain, particularly in areas responsible for executive function and emotion regulation. These findings highlight that ADHD's manifestations are deeply rooted in neurobiology, not whims of behavior that can be corrected simply by 'trying harder.'

Another critical aspect to understand is the spectrum nature of ADHD. The condition manifests uniquely across different individuals, influenced by a complex interplay of genetic, neurological, and environmental factors. For some, impulsivity might be the most challenging aspect, while for others, time management might be the most daunting hurdle. This variability means that management strategies must be highly personalized—what works for one person may not work for another. Recognizing this spectrum is vital for developing effective support and interventions that are tailored to individual needs, rather than adopting a one-size-fits-all approach.

Empowering through education is perhaps our most potent tool in this endeavor. Educating oneself about ADHD, understanding the nuances of its manifestation, and staying updated on the latest research can transform how one navigates the condition. Moreover, by sharing this knowledge with others—whether through conversations, workshops, or social media—we foster a more informed and empathetic society. This dissemination of knowledge not only combats stigma but also enriches the support network for those affected, creating communities that uplift rather than undermine.

In this landscape of understanding ADHD, we move beyond mere awareness to a profound comprehension that can significantly alter perceptions and interactions. By debunking myths, grounding our understanding in science, acknowledging the spectrum of symptoms, and actively educating ourselves and others, we not only enhance the lives of those directly affected by ADHD but also enrich our collective social fabric.

As this chapter closes, reflecting on the journey through the myths and realities of ADHD underscores the power of knowledge and the importance of empathy. It connects us to a broader narrative about the value of understanding and the impact of awareness in transforming lives. As we transition to the next chapter, the focus shifts to practical strategies and everyday applications, building on the foundation of understanding laid here to navigate ADHD with skill and confidence. This continuous thread of learning and applying, of knowing and doing, stitches together a tapestry of support and empowerment that can define the ADHD experience not just as manageable, but as deeply enriched.

Chapter 3: Mastering Focus and Productivity

I magine your workspace not just as a place where you conduct your tasks, but as a craftsman's workshop where every tool and setup is thoughtfully arranged to enhance creativity and efficiency. For adult men with ADHD, configuring your workspace isn't just about aesthetic appeal or conventional functionality—it's about creating an environment that actively supports your unique way of processing information and managing tasks. This chapter is dedicated to transforming your workspace into a haven that minimizes distractions and maximizes your productivity, tailored specifically to align with the ADHD brain.

Designing an ADHD-Friendly Workspace: Tips and Tools

Ergonomic Arrangements for Focus

The physical setup of your workspace can significantly impact your ability to focus and stay engaged. Ergonomics isn't just about comfort; it's about creating an environment that can help sustain your concentration and minimize physical strain that could lead to mental fatigue. Start with your chair: it should support your spine comfortably, promoting good posture to prevent the kind of discomfort that can distract you. The height of your desk and the position of your computer screen should encourage a natural line of sight, preventing neck strain. Consider a standing desk option, which can be particularly useful for when restlessness kicks in, allowing you to channel that energy without stepping away from your tasks. The freedom to alternate between sitting and standing can also help manage ADHD symptoms related to hyperactivity and the need for physical movement.

Clutter-Free Environment

A cluttered desk can lead to a cluttered mind, especially when you have ADHD. Visual noise can pull your attention away from tasks that require sustained focus. Begin by defining what is essential for your daily tasks and eliminate or store away everything else. Use drawer organizers or desktop trays to keep necessary items within reach but orderly. Digital clutter can also be distracting, so apply the same principles to your computer desktop. Regularly clear out unnecessary files and keep your digital workspace as organized as your physical one. This doesn't mean your space has to be stark or devoid of personality—personal touches are important for making a space feel comfortable and stimulating, but they should not overwhelm.

Sensory Tools for Concentration

Sensory tools are often overlooked but can be incredibly effective in enhancing focus. Noise-canceling headphones are a game-changer in noisy environments or when you need to block out background chatter. They can be used with white noise or ADHD-friendly productivity music that doesn't distract but rather enhances concentration. Consider also the tactile dimension of your workspace: objects like stress balls or fidget tools can allow you to expend excess energy without disrupting your workflow. These tools can help manage ADHD symptoms that manifest physically, providing an outlet for restlessness in a manner that maintains productivity.

Natural Elements and Productivity

Incorporating natural elements into your workspace can boost your mental well-being and focus. Natural light is particularly beneficial; it not only helps in reducing eye strain from artificial lighting but also enhances mood and energy levels. If possible, position your desk near a source of natural light or use daylight-simulating lamps if natural light isn't available. Adding plants to your workspace can also have a calming effect, improving air quality and providing a touch of nature that can be soothing for the ADHD mind. Select low-maintenance plants that don't require too much care, ensuring they enrich your environment without becoming a distraction.

Visual Aids for Task Management

Integrating visual aids into your workspace can play a crucial role in keeping you organized and focused. Visual cues act as constant reminders of tasks and deadlines, helping to overcome forgetfulness or the out-of-sight, out-of-mind challenges that are common with ADHD. Use whiteboards or corkboards to pin important notes, deadlines, or motivational quotes that keep you aligned with your goals. Color-coding tasks and using visual project tracking tools like Kanban boards can also provide clarity at a glance, breaking down projects into manageable parts and visually tracking progress.

In crafting an ADHD-friendly workspace, the goal is to minimize the elements that lead to sensory overload and distraction while enhancing those that support focus and productivity. This personalized approach to workspace design not only caters to your unique needs but also transforms your work area into a dynamic space conducive to creativity and efficiency. As you fine-tune your environment, you may find that the space where you work can significantly influence how well you work, turning it into a powerful ally in mastering focus and productivity.

The Power of Pomodoro and Other Time Management Techniques

Let's talk about the Pomodoro Technique, a time management method that is surprisingly effective, especially if you find yourself battling the unique time perception challenges that come with ADHD. Imagine breaking your workday into short sprints of productivity, followed by brief intervals of rest. This is the essence of the Pomodoro Technique, developed by Francesco Cirillo in the late 1980s. It's straightforward: you work for 25 minutes, then take a five-minute break. These intervals are known as "Pomodoros." After completing four Pomodoros, you take a longer break, around 15 to 30 minutes. This method is particularly beneficial for the ADHD brain, which might struggle with prolonged focus. It creates a rhythm that encourages sustained concentration but allows for the frequent breaks necessary to prevent mental fatigue. The work intervals are short enough to maintain a high level of focus without feeling overwhelming, and the breaks provide just enough time to reset and prepare for the next burst of activity. Additionally, this technique can help in reducing the anxiety associated with large, complex tasks by breaking the work into more manageable segments.

Time boxing is another technique that can revolutionize how you manage tasks, particularly if you tend to hyperfocus or procrastinate—two common challenges for men with ADHD. Time boxing involves allocating a fixed time period, a "box," to a specific activity or task before you start. For example, you might decide to spend only one hour on emails in the morning or set aside two hours in the afternoon for a project. This method helps limit the time you might otherwise spend over-perfecting a task or wandering off into less critical activities. It's about setting clear boundaries and expectations for what you want to achieve within that time frame, making it easier to start tasks and move on from them as needed. It also aids in making your day predictable and structured, which can reduce the stress and decision fatigue associated with ADHD.

Breaking tasks into manageable pieces is crucial when you're faced with a project that feels as daunting as climbing a mountain. This approach can be particularly helpful by making each step achievable and less intimidating. Start by outlining the major components of the project, then break these down into smaller, actionable steps. Each step should be clear and concrete, such as "draft the introduction of the report" rather than "work on report." This method not only makes the task at hand seem more approachable but also provides a clear roadmap of progress. As you tick off each small task, you're building momentum and a sense of accomplishment, which can be incredibly motivating. This tactic also helps in maintaining focus, as working towards a small, defined goal is generally less overwhelming than facing a monolithic project without a clear start or end point.

The use of visual timers can complement these strategies effectively by providing a constant, visual reminder of the passage of time. This can be a game-changer if you struggle with time blindness, a common issue for adults with ADHD. Visual timers differ from traditional clocks in that they help you see time passing, which can make time feel more tangible. For instance, a digital timer that shows a red disc diminishing as time elapses can provide a clear indication of how much time is left on a Pomodoro or a time-boxed task. This can help keep you grounded in the present and more aware of the passage of time, enhancing your ability to manage it effectively. Visual timers can also be used to signal transitions between different tasks or breaks, helping you stick to the structured schedule that is so beneficial for managing ADHD symptoms.

Incorporating these time management techniques into your daily routine can significantly enhance your productivity and ability to manage ADHD symptoms. Each method offers a unique way of structuring time that can help mitigate common challenges such as procrastination, time blindness, and the overwhelming feeling that large projects can evoke. By experimenting with these techniques, you can discover what combination works best for you, creating a personalized approach to time management that plays to your strengths and accommodates your challenges.

Leveraging Technology: Apps and Tools for Focus

In today's digital age, where technology is at your fingertips, it becomes a vital ally in managing ADHD, particularly when it comes to enhancing focus, time management, and task prioritization. The right set of apps and tools can transform your smartphone or computer from a source of distraction into a productivity powerhouse. Let's explore several technology solutions that can be specifically beneficial for you as an adult man with ADHD, aiming to streamline your daily activities and optimize your focus.

App Recommendations for Productivity

Navigating the vast sea of productivity apps available can be overwhelming, so here's a curated list of tools designed to enhance focus and efficiency. One such tool is 'Forest,' an app that encourages you to stay focused by growing a virtual tree which gradually grows as you work and dies if you leave the app to check your phone. This visual representation of your focus can be incredibly motivating. Another essential app is 'Todoist,' a powerful task manager that allows you to capture and organize tasks the moment they pop into your head. It enables you to set reminders, prioritize tasks using color codes, and even delegate tasks to others, making it invaluable for managing both personal and professional projects. For those who struggle with maintaining concentration over longer periods, 'Focus@Will' offers a solution by providing a selection of music scientifically optimized to boost concentration and minimize distractions.

Each of these apps addresses different aspects of ADHD-related challenges. By integrating them into your daily routine, you can harness technology to create a structured, distraction-minimized environment that supports sustained focus and productivity. Experiment with these tools to discover which combinations best suit your specific needs and preferences, and don't hesitate to adjust your toolkit as your requirements evolve.

Customizing Notifications to Reduce Distractions

Your digital devices, while useful, can often become a primary source of distraction, particularly with constant notifications from emails, social media, and other apps. Managing these interruptions is crucial for maintaining focus. Start by auditing your current notification settings. Identify which apps send you notifications and determine whether they are necessary. Tools like 'Daywise' can batch your notifications, delivering them in scheduled bursts rather than allowing them to trickle in throughout the day, which helps in reducing distractions and improving focus.

For work-related communications, consider setting up VIP lists so that you're only notified about emails from key contacts. Most email and messaging apps allow you to customize notifications so that you're only alerted to high-priority messages. Additionally, using 'Do Not Disturb' modes during focus-intensive tasks can prevent interruptions, creating periods of deep work that can dramatically enhance your productivity. By customizing these settings, you create a digital environment that supports rather than undermines your focus.

Digital Tools for Mind Mapping

For visual thinkers, particularly those with ADHD, mind mapping can be an effective strategy for organizing thoughts and ideas. Digital tools like 'MindMeister' allow you to create, share, and manage complex mind maps with ease. These tools enable you to visually structure your thoughts, making it easier to see connections, expand on ideas, and organize your plans. The ability to add colors, links, and even documents makes these tools incredibly versatile, adapting to your project's needs, whether it's planning an event, outlining a book, or strategizing a business plan.

Mind maps can also be a dynamic tool for brainstorming sessions, whether you're working alone or as part of a team. They allow you to capture and organize your thoughts in real-time, which can be particularly helpful if your ADHD makes it difficult to keep track of sprawling ideas. The interactive nature of digital mind mapping tools also means you can easily adjust and refine your maps as your ideas develop, making them an excellent tool for ongoing projects.

The Role of Wearable Technology

Wearable technology has begun playing a pivotal role in managing ADHD symptoms, particularly in monitoring and improving focus and stress levels. Devices like the 'Fitbit' or 'Apple Watch' can track your physical activity and sleep patterns—both of which are crucial for cognitive function and overall mental health. More advanced features, such as heart rate monitoring, can help you identify stress responses and take action to calm down before stress interferes with your focus or productivity.

Additionally, newer models of these devices offer apps specifically designed to promote focus and mindfulness. For instance, the Apple Watch features the 'Breathe' app, which guides you through short breathing exercises that can help reduce stress and improve concentration. These exercises can be particularly beneficial when you feel overwhelmed or notice your focus waning. By incorporating these wearable technologies into your daily routine, you can gain better insight into your physical and emotional health, helping you manage your ADHD symptoms more effectively.

Leveraging technology in these ways shows that with the right tools and strategies, you can turn potential distractions into powerful allies in your quest for enhanced productivity and focus. As you integrate these technologies into your routine, remember that the goal is to find solutions that fit seamlessly into your life, enhancing your ability to manage tasks and maintain focus without adding complexity or stress.

The Art of Prioritization: Managing Tasks with ADHD

In the bustling rhythm of daily life, managing a to-do list can feel like trying to tame a whirlwind—especially when your brain operates on an ADHD wavelength. Prioritization is not just about choosing what to do first; it's about strategically identifying which tasks will make the most significant impact on your day or overall goals. This can be particularly challenging when every task seems urgent or when your focus shifts rapidly. The first step is to develop a keen eye for distinguishing between tasks that are truly crucial and those that are merely loud.

Identifying high-impact tasks involves more than recognizing what needs to be done; it requires understanding the potential outcomes of different tasks. Start by asking yourself: What are the consequences of not completing this task? If the answer points to significant negative impacts, such as missing a critical deadline or losing a valuable opportunity, then it's a high-impact task. Another useful approach is to consider which tasks will bring you closer to your personal or professional goals. This aligns your daily activities with your longer-term ambitions, ensuring that your efforts are not just productive but also progressive. Remember, high-impact tasks aren't necessarily the most time-consuming or the most complex; they are the ones that will have the most substantial effect on your progress.

The Eisenhower Matrix, a time-tested method of task prioritization, can be particularly effective for individuals with ADHD. It helps categorize tasks into four quadrants based on urgency and importance: urgent and important, not urgent but important, urgent but not important, and neither urgent nor important. For someone with ADHD, the challenge often lies in not getting swept away by the 'urgent but not important' tasks, which can be distracting and detract from more meaningful activities. Adapting this matrix to your use involves a clear and honest assessment of what 'urgent' and 'important' mean in the context of your life and goals. It also means being disciplined about not letting the 'urgent' overshadow the 'important,' which is a common pitfall when you're feeling pressured.

Setting realistic deadlines is another critical component of effective task management with ADHD. The perception of time can sometimes be skewed, and traditional deadlines can seem either intimidating or irrelevant until they're alarmingly close. To counter this, start by breaking down projects into smaller, manageable stages, each with its own deadline. This method, known as micro-deadlining, can help maintain a steady pace and avoid last-minute rushes. Be generous and realistic with your time estimates, considering potential distractions and the need for breaks. If possible, build in buffer periods to accommodate the unexpected—a common occurrence in the life of someone with ADHD. This flexibility can reduce the stress and anxiety often associated with deadlines and help maintain a steady flow of productivity.

Establishing daily planning rituals can significantly enhance your ability to stay on top of priorities and adapt to changing circumstances. This might involve setting aside time each morning to review your tasks for the day or each evening to plan for the next. During this ritual, assess what was accomplished, what wasn't, and why. This reflection not only helps you stay aligned with your goals but also improves your understanding of how you work best. Use tools that resonate with your style, whether it's a digital planner, a classic paper notebook, or an app that syncs across all your devices. The key is consistency and the willingness to adjust your plans as needed, allowing you to navigate each day with clarity and focus.

Mastering the art of prioritization when you have ADHD involves a blend of self-awareness, strategic planning, and adaptability. It's about making informed choices that align your daily actions with your bigger picture, transforming the chaos of countless tasks into a structured ladder leading towards your goals. As you become more adept at recognizing high-impact tasks, using tools like the Eisenhower Matrix effectively, setting realistic deadlines, and establishing productive planning rituals, you'll find that managing tasks becomes less of a battle and more of a balanced dance. This skill not only enhances your productivity but also empowers you to take charge of your time and focus, turning them into valuable assets in your pursuit of success and satisfaction.

Building and Maintaining Momentum in Projects

Initiating a new project can often feel like standing at the base of a steep mountain. It's not just the physical act of starting that's daunting—it's also the mental preparation required to take that first step. For adults with ADHD, this initial hurdle can be particularly challenging due to tendencies toward procrastination or overwhelm by the scale of the task at hand. One effective method to overcome this is to break the project into extremely small, manageable actions. For instance, if the project is to write a report, the first action might be as simple as opening your computer and creating a new document named after the report. This might seem overly simplistic, but the act of starting can significantly reduce the mental barrier to entry. The key is to make the first step so easy that it's almost harder not to do it than to do it.

Once the project is underway, maintaining momentum can be another challenge, especially when faced with the inevitable ups and downs that accompany any significant endeavor. ADHD can complicate this further, with fluctuating motivation levels and a heightened sensitivity to setbacks. To keep the momentum, it's crucial to set up short-term goals or checkpoints throughout the project. These act not only as markers of progress but also as regular injections of motivation. Additionally, employing a technique known as "temptation bundling" can prove beneficial. This involves linking a task you need to do (like working on a project) with an activity you enjoy (such as listening to your favorite podcast). The pleasure associated with the enjoyable activity can help fuel your motivation to engage in the less appealing task, making it easier to maintain momentum.

Celebrating milestones is not just a way to mark progress—it's a vital strategy in acknowledging your hard work and reinforcing your motivation. This is particularly important for ADHD, where external affirmations can significantly boost self-esteem and motivation. Make a habit of celebrating all victories, big and small. Did you complete the first section of your report? That's an achievement. Treat yourself to a coffee break, a short walk, or another small reward. These celebrations can serve as positive reinforcement, making the journey more enjoyable and sustainable. They remind you that progress, no matter how incremental, is still progress.

Dealing with project fatigue—when enthusiasm and energy wane—is a common experience, and for someone with ADHD, this fatigue can hit harder and disrupt momentum more significantly. One strategy to combat this is by scheduling regular reviews of why you started the project in the first place. Reconnecting with your initial motivation can reignite your passion. Also, changing your environment can refresh your perspective. This could mean working from a different location, rearranging your workspace, or even just altering your work schedule to allow some flexibility. Sometimes, introducing a new tool or method for completing the project tasks can also provide a novel twist that renews interest.

Maintaining momentum in projects when you have ADHD involves a dynamic mix of strategies tailored to your unique needs and responses. By understanding and implementing these strategies, you can transform the way you handle projects from start to finish—turning potential stumbling blocks into stepping stones towards successful project completion. These techniques not only enhance your productivity but also contribute to a more fulfilling and enjoyable work process, aligning your efforts with your goals in a meaningful way.

In wrapping up this chapter on mastering focus and productivity, we've explored a variety of strategies from designing an ADHD-friendly workspace to leveraging technology and maintaining project momentum. Each of these strategies is aimed at optimizing your work environment and methods to suit your unique brain wiring, enhancing both your efficiency and your job satisfaction. As we transition into the next chapter, we will delve into navigating personal relationships, an integral part of personal and professional life, which presents its own set of challenges and opportunities for adults with ADHD. Here, the focus will shift from enhancing personal productivity to fostering interpersonal connections, understanding how ADHD can impact relationships, and exploring strategies to build and maintain healthy interactions.

Chapter 4: Navigating Personal Relationships

I n the realm of personal relationships, navigating the waters can often feel turbulent, especially when you're steering with the unique oar of ADHD. Relationships require a balance of give and take, understanding, and communication—elements that can be inherently more challenging with ADHD. But consider this: the skills and tools you've honed to manage your ADHD can also be your greatest allies in enhancing your relationships. This chapter aims to transform your approach to relationships, providing you with strategies not only to sustain but to strengthen your connections with others.

Communication Strategies That Strengthen Relationships

Active Listening Techniques

In the tapestry of relationships, active listening is the thread that strengthens the weave, binding individuals together through the power of understanding. For men with ADHD, mastering this skill can be particularly transformative. Active listening involves fully concentrating on the speaker, understanding their message, responding thoughtfully, and remembering the information shared. It's more than just hearing words; it's about engaging with and processing the emotions and meanings behind them. To practice active listening, start by minimizing distractions—turn off the TV, put away your phone, and focus entirely on the conversation. Use nonverbal cues like nodding or maintaining eye contact to show engagement. Repeat back what you've heard in your own words to confirm understanding, a technique known as reflective listening. This not only shows that you are paying attention but also helps clarify any miscommunication right at the moment. By enhancing your active listening skills, you open new avenues of connection and understanding, making your interactions richer and more meaningful.

Expressing Needs Clearly

Articulating your needs and desires in a relationship can sometimes feel like navigating a minefield, especially when emotions are high. However, clear communication is the cornerstone of healthy relationships. For adults with ADHD, who might struggle with impulsivity or disorganization, this can be particularly challenging. Start by identifying your needs clearly in your own mind before attempting to communicate them to others. It might help to write them down first. When you're ready to express these needs, use "I" statements to frame your thoughts, such as "I feel" or "I need," instead of "You never" or "You always." This approach reduces the likelihood of sounding accusatory and increases the chances that your words will be received with openness rather than defensiveness. Be specific about what you need, why it's important to you, and how you and your partner can work together to meet this need. This clarity not only helps prevent misunderstandings but also fosters cooperation and support.

Navigating Misunderstandings

Misunderstandings are inevitable in any relationship, but they don't have to derail it. When conflicts arise, especially for those with ADHD who might experience heightened emotions or impulsivity, it's crucial to approach resolution constructively. Take a step back and allow yourself time to cool down if emotions run high. Approach the situation with a mindset of resolution, not confrontation. Discuss one issue at a time instead of bringing up past grievances. Use clear, calm language and refer to specific behaviors rather than generalizing. Remember, the goal is not to win an argument but to understand each other better and strengthen the relationship. By developing strategies to navigate misunderstandings effectively, you transform potential conflicts into opportunities for growth and deeper connection.

The Role of Nonverbal Communication

Nonverbal cues often speak louder than words, especially in emotional exchanges. For men with ADHD, who may sometimes miss these subtle cues, understanding and using nonverbal communication effectively can significantly enhance relationships. Nonverbal communication includes facial expressions, body language, gestures, eye contact, tone of voice, and even your physical space or how close you stand to someone. To improve your nonverbal communication skills, start by becoming more aware of your own body language and what it might be conveying. Ensure your facial expressions match the message you're trying to communicate. Maintain appropriate eye contact to show interest and sincerity. Be mindful of your tone of voice, as it can convey emotions more powerfully than the words themselves. By aligning your verbal and nonverbal cues, you enhance your ability to communicate effectively, ensuring that your message is understood as intended.

Developing robust communication strategies is essential for maintaining and strengthening relationships. By mastering active listening, expressing your needs clearly, navigating misunderstandings with grace, and understanding the power of nonverbal cues, you equip yourself with the tools to build deeper, more meaningful connections. These skills foster a greater understanding and appreciation between you and your loved ones, enhancing the quality of your interactions and the strength of your bonds.

Understanding and Navigating Emotional Responses

Navigating the emotional landscape of relationships can often feel like steering a ship through stormy seas, especially when ADHD is part of the equation. Emotional responses can be swift and intense, and understanding how to manage these effectively is crucial for maintaining healthy relationships. Recognizing emotional triggers is the first step in this process. Emotional triggers are specific events or interactions that elicit strong emotional reactions. These can vary widely from one person to another but often include feelings of being overwhelmed, criticized, or ignored. For someone with ADHD, these triggers might also be tied to experiences of past failures or rejections, which can amplify the emotional response. Identifying these triggers involves a mix of self-reflection and observation. Keeping a journal can be an invaluable tool here; it allows you to record instances where your emotions felt out of control and to reflect on what might have sparked these feelings. Over time, patterns can emerge that help pinpoint specific triggers, making them easier to manage or avoid in the future.

Once triggers are identified, developing strategies for emotion regulation is essential. Emotion regulation doesn't mean suppressing your feelings; rather, it involves understanding them and responding in ways that are proportionate and constructive. Techniques such as deep breathing, mindfulness, and pausing before responding can help manage immediate emotional impulses. For example, when a trigger is recognized, taking a few deep breaths can help slow down the physiological response, giving you time to process the emotion more rationally. Another effective strategy is the use of grounding techniques, which help draw attention away from distressing emotions and back to the present moment. This could be as simple as focusing on the physical sensations of your feet on the ground or the sounds around you, helping to break the cycle of escalating emotions.

ADHD can significantly impact emotional intimacy—the feelings of closeness and connectedness with a partner. This aspect of relationships relies heavily on emotional give and take, which can be complicated by the impulsivity and emotional sensitivity associated with ADHD. To enhance emotional intimacy, it's important to create a safe space where both partners feel they can share their feelings openly and without judgment. Regular check-ins can be beneficial, providing a structured opportunity to discuss feelings and concerns. During these times, practicing active empathy by really listening to your partner's experiences without immediately offering solutions or dismissals can strengthen the emotional bond. It's also helpful to share your own experiences with ADHD, explaining how it might affect your reactions and emotions. This open line of communication can foster greater understanding and patience between partners, deepening the emotional connection.

In situations where emotional challenges become too complex to manage alone, seeking professional help can be a wise course of action. Couples therapy, for example, can provide a neutral space to explore emotional difficulties with the guidance of a trained professional. Therapists who specialize in ADHD can offer insights not only into managing individual symptoms but also in how these symptoms interact within the relationship dynamics. They can introduce techniques and exercises designed to improve communication, increase empathy, and strengthen emotional connections. Additionally, individual therapy can also be beneficial, providing a space to explore personal emotional triggers and regulation strategies in depth, without the immediate pressures of relationship dynamics.

Navigating emotional responses in relationships requires a balanced approach of self-awareness, communication, and sometimes, professional guidance. By understanding and managing your emotional triggers, employing effective regulation strategies, and enhancing emotional intimacy, you can create a more stable and fulfilling relationship. Moreover, recognizing when to seek help and taking steps to engage in therapy can provide the tools and support needed to navigate more complex emotional landscapes, ultimately leading to healthier and more resilient partnerships.

ADHD and Intimacy: Building Closer Bonds

Understanding the interplay between ADHD and intimacy illuminates the unique challenges that can emerge in relationships, whether they are emotional or physical. The intensity and unpredictability of emotions that often accompany ADHD can make intimate connections both incredibly rewarding and, at times, complex. For instance, the spontaneity and energy brought into a relationship by someone with ADHD can invigorate it, infusing it with life and excitement. However, the same traits might lead to inconsistencies in emotional availability or responsiveness, which can pose challenges for building a steady, intimate bond. This dual nature necessitates a deeper understanding and strategic approaches to nurturing intimacy.

Navigating intimacy with ADHD involves more than managing symptoms; it requires an understanding of how these symptoms affect both partners in the relationship. Communication lapses, for instance, can lead to feelings of neglect or misunderstanding. The distractibility characteristic of ADHD might mean missing subtle cues that a partner is seeking emotional connection or support, which can lead to feelings of isolation or rejection. On the other hand, impulsivity might result in spontaneous decisions that can upset a relationship's balance, such as unplanned expenditures or last-minute changes to shared plans. By recognizing these potential pitfalls, you can begin to construct strategies that mitigate their impact, such as setting aside specific times for undistracted conversation or planning for spontaneity in a way that includes mutual decision-making.

Enhancing emotional intimacy in relationships where one or both partners have ADHD can be particularly rewarding. It starts with openness about the challenges and how they manifest in your relationship. Sharing your experiences with ADHD, discussing how it affects your emotions and reactions, and allowing your partner to share their feelings and experiences creates a foundation of mutual understanding and empathy. This transparency can foster a deeper connection, as both partners feel seen and understood on a fundamental level. Moreover, engaging in shared activities that encourage connection can be beneficial. Whether it's a regular date night, a shared hobby, or simply a nightly routine of discussing the day's highs and lows, these activities can strengthen emotional bonds by creating shared experiences and opportunities for emotional support.

Physical intimacy can also be influenced by ADHD in ways that are not immediately obvious. Variabilities in attention can affect one's ability to stay present during intimate moments, which can be perceived as a lack of interest or affection. Furthermore, the medication used to manage ADHD symptoms can sometimes have side effects that affect sexual health and desire. Addressing these issues openly with your partner, and possibly with a healthcare provider, can help both partners understand these challenges and explore solutions or adjustments to treatment that consider both partners' needs. Regular, open discussions about physical needs and desires, comfort levels, and affectionate gestures can enhance physical intimacy, making both partners feel desired and valued.

Building a partnership mindset shifts the approach in a relationship from navigating individual challenges to tackling them together as a unified team. This perspective encourages both partners to support each other's growth and well-being, recognizing that the health of the relationship directly impacts each individual's health. In practice, this means actively working to understand how ADHD affects each partner and the relationship as a whole, and collaboratively finding strategies that enhance life together. It involves regularly checking in on each other's well-being, celebrating successes, and addressing challenges proactively. By fostering this collaborative approach, the relationship can become a powerful, supportive framework, wherein both partners feel they are working together towards common goals, rather than struggling alone or against each other. This partnership mindset not only strengthens the bond but also creates a resilient foundation that can withstand the challenges that come with ADHD.

Navigating the intricate dynamics of intimacy when you or your partner has ADHD requires patience, understanding, and a proactive approach to fostering connection. By embracing strategies that enhance both emotional and physical intimacy and adopting a partnership mindset, you can build a relationship that is not only resilient but also deeply fulfilling.

Setting Boundaries: Strategies for Healthy Relationships

Understanding the critical role of boundaries in relationships is like recognizing the need for rules in a sport—it defines how the game is played, ensuring that all participants enjoy the experience without detriment to each other. Particularly for those with ADHD, where impulsivity, emotion regulation challenges, and difficulty in managing time can strain relationships, setting clear boundaries is essential. These boundaries help in managing expectations and fostering a respectful and supportive interaction, both of which are crucial for maintaining healthy relationships. They serve as guidelines that help you understand where you end and where another person begins, ensuring that your needs and the needs of others are mutually respected and met.

Identifying personal boundaries is the first step in this essential process. It involves a deep and honest reflection on what you are comfortable with, how much you can handle emotionally and mentally, and where you draw the line. This might include limits on how much personal information you share, how you want to be treated by others, and what kind of commitments you can realistically manage. For someone with ADHD, this might mean setting boundaries around time management, such as not accepting phone calls during work hours to maintain focus, or around emotional expenditure, like choosing not to engage in discussions when overly stressed. Writing these boundaries down can help clarify them for yourself before you communicate them to others.

Effective communication of your boundaries is crucial. It involves expressing your limits clearly, calmly, and assertively to those involved. This is not about making demands or ultimatums but about expressing your needs respectfully and openly. For example, if you're uncomfortable with last-minute changes to plans, you might say, "I feel stressed when plans change suddenly without warning. I'd appreciate it if we could stick to the scheduled plans or discuss changes well in advance." This kind of communication not only helps in setting clear expectations but also minimizes the likelihood of misunderstandings and conflicts. It's also important to be consistent in enforcing these boundaries once they are set, as this consistency helps others understand the seriousness of your needs and respect them accordingly.

Respecting others' boundaries is just as crucial as setting your own. This involves actively listening when others express their limits and making a conscious effort to honor them. For example, if a friend mentions they are not taking calls after 8 PM because they need time to unwind, respecting this boundary is essential. It shows that you value their needs and are willing to support their well-being. In relationships where ADHD is present, being mindful of how your actions affect others—whether it's acknowledging their need for quiet time or recognizing their limits on spontaneous activities—can significantly enhance mutual understanding and respect.

Individuals with ADHD might face unique challenges in setting and respecting boundaries due to symptoms like impulsivity and forgetfulness. These challenges can sometimes lead to crossing others' boundaries without intention or struggling to maintain their own. Strategies to manage these challenges include using reminders or setting up systems that help keep track of commitments and boundaries.

For instance, setting alarms as reminders for time-sensitive boundaries or having a visual chart that helps keep track of weekly commitments can be useful tools. Additionally, regular check-ins with loved ones about these boundaries can help maintain them effectively, providing an opportunity to adjust as needed and ensure that all parties feel respected and understood.

In sum, setting and respecting boundaries are fundamental to cultivating healthy, balanced relationships. They help manage expectations, reduce conflicts, and build a foundation of respect and understanding. For adults with ADHD, while the challenge may be greater, the strategies mentioned can offer a roadmap to better manage these dynamics. By actively engaging in setting, communicating, and respecting boundaries, you not only enhance your personal relationships but also improve your overall well-being and the well-being of those around you.

Transitioning from navigating personal relationships, the next chapter will delve into financial management and impulsivity. Here, we'll explore how ADHD can impact financial decisions and what strategies can be employed to manage finances effectively, ensuring financial stability and reducing stress related to monetary matters. This shift from interpersonal dynamics to financial management highlights the broad spectrum of areas affected by ADHD and underscores the importance of comprehensive strategies to manage these effects holistically.

CHAPTER 5: FINANCIAL MANAGEMENT AND IMPULSIVITY

Imagine standing in the electronics store, eyes locked on the latest smartphone model. It's sleek, fast, and has the most cutting-edge technology. You feel the itch of impulse, the rush of desire to own it, the thrill of purchasing something new. Yet, in the back of your mind, there's a nagging thought about your budget and financial priorities. This scenario is all too familiar for many men with ADHD, where impulsivity doesn't just extend to actions or words but also to financial decisions. Managing money requires structure and foresight—attributes that can sometimes be overshadowed by the immediacy of wants and the challenge of delayed gratification associated with ADHD. This chapter is dedicated to turning the tide on financial impulsivity, offering strategies that not only align with your financial goals but also respect the unique challenges of your neurodiverse mind.

Budgeting With an ADHD Brain: Making It Stick

ADHD-Friendly Budgeting Methods

The cornerstone of sound financial management is effective budgeting, yet the traditional methods of tracking every penny can be overwhelming if you have ADHD. It's essential to find a method that resonates with your lifestyle and cognitive patterns. One effective approach is the use of digital budgeting tools that simplify the tracking process and provide visual feedback on your spending habits. Apps like Mint or YNAB (You Need A Budget) can be particularly helpful.

They automatically categorize your expenses and visually represent your spending against your budget limits, making it easier to see where your money goes without needing to dig through bank statements. These tools are especially useful if you struggle with organization and forgetfulness, common ADHD traits, as they keep your financial overview accessible and straightforward.

Another ADHD-friendly budgeting method involves simplifying your budget into larger categories rather than micro-managing every expense. Instead of detailed classifications, you might have broad categories like 'Bills,' 'Food,' 'Transportation,' and 'Entertainment.' This reduces the cognitive load required to categorize each expense and makes the process less daunting. Additionally, setting up automatic transfers to different accounts can help manage spending. For example, having separate accounts for daily expenses, savings, and bills, where portions of your income are automatically directed, can prevent the risk of overspending.

The Role of Automation in Financial Management

Automation is a powerful ally in managing finances, especially for individuals with ADHD. It reduces the number of decisions you need to make about where and when money should be allocated, which can be a relief if decision fatigue is a common issue. Setting up automatic payments for recurring bills ensures that they are paid on time, helping avoid late fees and the stress associated with missed payments. Similarly, automatic savings plans can help you build a savings buffer without needing to remember to transfer money each month. By automating these financial tasks, you create a safety net that protects against impulsive spending and ensures that your financial responsibilities are met consistently.

Visualizing Financial Goals

For many with ADHD, long-term goals can sometimes feel abstract and difficult to connect with daily actions. Visualizing these goals can make them more tangible and motivating. Consider using visual tools like charts or vision boards where you map out your financial goals with images and diagrams. For instance, if you're saving for a vacation, you could have a picture of the destination along with a savings tracker that you update regularly. This not only makes the goal feel more real but also provides a visual reminder of your progress, which can be incredibly satisfying and motivating.

Creating an Emergency Fund

Impulsivity can often lead to unexpected spending, which might interfere with your financial stability. Creating an emergency fund is crucial as it provides a financial cushion that can absorb unforeseen expenses without derailing your budget. Start small, aiming to save a manageable amount each month, and gradually build this fund over time. The key is consistency rather than the amount. Having this fund not only reduces stress associated with unexpected financial demands but also reduces the temptation to make impulsive financial decisions since you know you have a backup.

By integrating these strategies into your financial management routines, you can create a framework that accommodates the unique challenges of ADHD, turning potential impulsivity into a structured, goal-oriented financial plan. This approach not only ensures stability and progress towards your financial goals but also empowers you to handle your finances with confidence, making each decision a stepping stone towards greater financial independence and security.

Tools and Techniques to Curb Impulsive Spending

Understanding and managing the triggers that lead to impulsive spending can significantly enhance your financial control, especially when dealing with ADHD. Impulsive spending often occurs in response to emotional triggers such as stress, excitement, or even boredom. For someone with ADHD, the immediacy of the gratification from impulsive purchases can be particularly seductive, overshadowing longer-term financial goals. The first step in curbing this tendency is to identify what prompts these impulses. Do you find yourself reaching for your wallet when you're feeling low to give yourself a lift? Or perhaps when you're elated, do you celebrate by spending? Keeping a spending diary can be an enlightening way to track these patterns. Over a month, jot down each purchase along with what you were feeling at the time you made it. Patterns will likely emerge that link your emotions to your spending habits, offering crucial insights into your personal triggers.

Once these triggers are identified, developing strategies to manage them becomes possible. For instance, if stress leads you to shop, finding alternative stress-relief methods like exercise, meditation, or engaging in a hobby can mitigate this trigger. Setting a waiting period for purchases is another effective strategy. Implementing a 24-hour rule before buying non-essential items gives you time to consider if the purchase is necessary or just a response to a fleeting feeling. This pause can often dampen the impulse, aligning your actions more closely with your financial goals.

The envelope system is a classic budgeting technique that offers a tangible way to manage spending across different categories. It works by dividing your cash for the month into envelopes, each labeled for a specific spending area like groceries, entertainment, or dining out. Once the cash in any envelope is gone, spending in that category is paused until the next refill cycle. This method provides a visual and physical representation of your budget, making it easier to see and feel your spending. It can be particularly effective if digital spending feels abstract and uncontrollable. The tactile nature of handling real money can make the impact of spending more concrete, thus enhancing mindfulness in financial decisions.

Mindful spending is about creating a more intentional relationship with your money. It involves pausing to ask yourself several questions before making a purchase: Do I need this? Why do I want this? How will this purchase impact my financial goals? This practice fosters a deeper awareness of the difference between wants and needs, helping to resist impulsive purchases. For someone with ADHD, who might struggle with impulsivity, inculcating a habit of mindful spending can transform financial habits profoundly. It shifts spending from an automatic, often regrettable reaction to a deliberate, satisfying decision.

Technology also offers powerful tools to aid in managing and controlling spending. Several apps are designed to alert you when you're about to exceed your budget or when you make an unusually large transaction. Apps like Mint provide real-time updates on your spending relative to your budget, while others like PocketGuard can even lock identified overspending categories once their limit is reached. These apps not only track spending but also analyze your habits, offering insights that can lead to more tailored and effective spending strategies. Setting up alerts for when your bank account drops below a certain threshold can also prevent overdraft fees and help maintain a buffer against impulsive spending.

By utilizing these tools and techniques, you can develop a robust framework to manage your finances more effectively, keeping impulsive spending in check and aligning your daily financial decisions with your long-term financial health and goals. This proactive approach not only secures your financial well-being but also empowers you to handle your finances with confidence, knowing that you have the strategies and supports in place to maintain control.

Planning for the Future: ADHD-Friendly Financial Advice

When you think about the future, it might feel like looking through a foggy window, murky and undefined. This is especially true if you're dealing with ADHD, where the future often takes a backseat to the immediacy of now. Yet, planning for the future is crucial, not just to secure your financial well-being, but also to give you peace of mind and a sense of control. Long-term financial planning might sound daunting, but with the right strategies, it can become a structured and rewarding process. Start by setting clear, achievable goals. Whether it's saving for a down payment on a house, planning a dream vacation, or preparing for retirement, having specific targets gives you something concrete to work towards. Use visual aids like charts or apps that track your progress towards these goals. Seeing a visual representation of your savings growing can provide a motivational boost and a tangible reminder of what you're working towards.

It's also helpful to automate your savings. Set up automatic transfers to a dedicated savings account or a retirement fund at the beginning of each month, treating it like any other non-negotiable expense.

This not only ensures that you consistently save but also reduces the temptation to spend what you may perceive as available money. For those with ADHD, who might struggle with impulsivity and maintaining financial consistency, this method ensures that your future goals are being funded before everyday spending decisions come into play. Additionally, consider revisiting and adjusting these goals annually or when major life events occur. This keeps your financial plan flexible and relevant to your current life circumstances, accommodating for changes in income, lifestyle, or financial obligations.

Investing might seem like a territory marked with complex charts and unpredictable markets, which can be intimidating if you prefer simplicity and minimal maintenance in your financial dealings. However, investing is a crucial component of long-term financial planning, offering potential growth that savings accounts rarely match. Start with low-maintenance investment options. Mutual funds, particularly index funds, are a great choice as they offer diversified investments without the need for constant monitoring or trading. These funds replicate the performance of a specific index, like the S&P 500, meaning they are designed to mirror the market's performance, generally requiring less oversight and yielding steady growth over time.

For those with ADHD, who might find the fluctuations of the stock market stressful, consider setting up a robo-advisor account. Robo-advisors use algorithms to manage your investments based on your risk tolerance and financial goals. They automatically adjust your portfolio to optimize for the best potential return, which can be a relief if you find the idea of manually rebalancing your investments overwhelming. Additionally, these platforms often allow you to set up automatic contributions, further simplifying the investment process. It's a way to make your money work for you, without necessitating daily or even monthly involvement, which can be particularly advantageous for maintaining focus on your current financial and personal obligations.

Protecting against financial vulnerabilities is also a critical aspect of long-term financial planning, especially for those with ADHD. Impulsivity and variable income are just a couple of the challenges you might face. One way to safeguard against these vulnerabilities is through insurance and emergency funds. Make sure you have comprehensive health insurance, disability insurance, and an emergency fund that covers at least three to six months of living expenses. These safety nets ensure that you're prepared for unexpected health issues or sudden income disruptions, which can otherwise cause significant financial strain. For those with ADHD, who might find themselves switching jobs more frequently or encountering unexpected expenses due to impulsivity, such protection is not just helpful, it's essential for maintaining long-term financial stability.

Seeking professional financial advice can be a game-changer in your journey toward financial security. Financial planners can offer personalized advice tailored to your unique circumstances, including your goals, challenges, and the nuances of managing finances with ADHD. They can help you devise a comprehensive financial plan that encompasses everything from daily budget management to long-term investment strategies. More importantly, they can provide accountability—a crucial element if you struggle with consistency in managing finances. A financial advisor can help you stay on track, making regular adjustments to your plan as needed and guiding you through complex financial decisions, ensuring that your financial health remains robust as you navigate the uncertainties of the future. Engaging a professional might seem like an additional expense, but consider it an investment in your financial well-being, offering you expertise and peace of mind as you build a secure financial foundation for the years to come.

Overcoming Debt: A Step-by-Step Guide for Men with ADHD

Understanding your debt and its various forms is crucial in managing it effectively. Debt isn't just a number; it's a financial obligation that can significantly impact your emotional and financial well-being. There are typically two main types of debt: secured and unsecured. Secured debts are those backed by an asset, like a house or car. Failure to pay can lead to the asset being taken as collateral. On the other hand, unsecured debts, like most credit cards and student loans, don't involve tangible assets but can still lead to substantial financial strain due to high interest rates and penalties for late payments. Each type of debt affects your financial health differently and understanding these nuances is key to developing a strategy to manage and eventually eliminate them.

One effective way to tackle debt is through structured repayment strategies such as the snowball and avalanche methods. The snowball method involves paying off debts from the smallest to the largest amount, regardless of interest rate. This method can be particularly motivating because you see debts disappearing quicker, which can be a significant psychological boost. It aligns well with the ADHD need for quick, visible results, helping maintain motivation. Conversely, the avalanche method focuses on paying off debts with the highest interest rates first, regardless of the debt amount. This method can save you money over time on interest payments. Both methods have their merits, and choosing the right one can depend on your personal preference for quick wins or overall efficiency.

Negotiating with creditors is another crucial strategy in managing your debts more effectively. It might seem daunting, but many creditors are willing to work with you to adjust your repayment terms. This can include lowering interest rates, waiving late fees, or restructuring the debt to lower monthly payments. When approaching creditors, it's beneficial to come prepared with a clear understanding of your financial situation and a realistic proposal for repayment. Be honest about your ADHD if it's relevant to your financial struggles, as this can sometimes help in gaining their sympathy and cooperation. Maintaining a polite and cooperative demeanor increases the likelihood of successful negotiations, helping you manage your debts more sustainably.

Maintaining motivation during the often lengthy process of debt repayment is critical. It's easy to feel discouraged, especially when progress seems slow, and balances are high. To keep your spirits up, set small, achievable milestones and celebrate when you reach them. These celebrations don't have to be extravagant but should remind you that you're making progress. Visual aids can also play a significant role here. Consider a debt repayment chart that you update monthly; watching the numbers decrease can provide a visual representation of your progress and help maintain your focus on the end goal. Additionally, consider joining support groups for people dealing with debt. Sharing your experiences and hearing others' stories can provide mutual encouragement and practical advice, making the journey less isolating.

As this chapter on overcoming debt concludes, remember the key points: understanding the types of debt, choosing a repayment strategy that suits your psychological needs, negotiating with creditors, and keeping motivated throughout the repayment process. These strategies are designed not just to help you manage and eliminate your debt but also to empower you with financial discipline that extends into all areas of your financial life. As we move forward, the next chapter will delve into the emotional regulation and stress management strategies that can further enhance your journey toward a more stable and fulfilling life, linking financial health with overall mental well-being.

Make a Difference with Your Review

Unlock the Power of Generosity

"The simplest acts of kindness are by far more powerful than a thousand heads bowing in prayer." - Mahatma Gandhi

People who give without expectation live longer, happier lives and make more money. So if we've got a shot at that during our time together, darn it, I'm gonna try.

To make that happen, I have a question for you...

Would you help someone you've never met, even if you never got credit for it?

Who is this person you ask? They are like you. Or, at least, like you used to be. Less experienced, wanting to make a difference, and needing help, but not sure where to look.

My mission is to make Adult ADHD advice accessible to everyone. Everything I do stems from that mission. And, the only way for me to accomplish that mission is by reaching...well...everyone.

This is where you come in. Most people do, in fact, judge a book by its cover (and its reviews). So here's my ask on behalf of a struggling man with ADHD you've never met:

Please help that man with ADHD by leaving this book a review.

Your gift costs no money and less than 60 seconds to make real, but can change a fellow man with ADHD's life forever. Your review could help...

- ...one more small business provide for their community.

- ...one more entrepreneur support their family.

- ...one more employee get meaningful work.

- ...one more client transform their life.

- ...one more dream come true.

To get that 'feel good' feeling and help this person for real, all you have to do is...and it takes less than 60 seconds... leave a review.

Simply scan the QR code below to leave your review:

If you feel good about helping a faceless man with ADHD, you are my kind of person. Welcome to the club. You're one of us.

I'm that much more excited to help you improve focus, increase productivity, and thrive in life faster than you can possibly imagine.

You'll love the strategies and exercises I'm about to share in the coming chapters.

Thank you from the bottom of my heart. Now, back to our regularly scheduled programming.

Your biggest fan, Mark Fitzgerald

PS - Fun fact: If you provide something of value to another person, it makes you more valuable to them. If you'd like goodwill straight from another man with ADHD - and you believe this book will help them - send this book their way.

Chapter 6 Emotional Regulation and Stress Management

I magine you're at the helm of a ship in the midst of a storm; waves crashing, winds howling. Now, imagine navigating this storm with the calm of a seasoned captain. This chapter is your guide to becoming that captain in the stormy seas of emotional regulation and stress management, particularly tailored for the unique challenges faced by adult men with ADHD.

Mindfulness Practices Tailored for the ADHD Mind

The Basics of Mindfulness

Mindfulness, the art of being present and fully engaged with the now, without distraction or judgment, can seem like a lofty goal, especially when your mind tends to race with a constant stream of thoughts. However, mindfulness for the ADHD mind isn't about silencing these thoughts; it's about learning to observe them without getting swept away. This begins with understanding that mindfulness isn't a 'one-size-fits-all' practice. It's about finding short, engaging practices that can fit into your daily routine and help you gradually increase your ability to focus and remain calm. For instance, start with what I like to call 'One-Minute Mindfulness' exercises. These involve focusing all your attention on a single, simple task for one minute, whether it's feeling the sensations of washing dishes or simply observing your breath. These brief moments of mindfulness can serve as a soothing anchor, bringing you back to the present and cutting through the noise of scattered thoughts.

Breathing Exercises

One of the most powerful tools in your mindfulness toolkit is something you carry with you at all times: your breath. Breathing exercises are a quick way to center yourself and bring your focus back from the pull of past regrets or future anxieties. A technique particularly effective for the ADHD mind is the 4-4-8 breathing method. Here's how it works: breathe in deeply through your nose for four seconds, hold that breath for another four seconds, and then exhale slowly through your mouth for eight seconds. This method not only helps in reducing the physical symptoms of stress but also aids in slowing down racing thoughts, making it easier to focus on the task at hand.

Mindful Movement

For many with ADHD, traditional meditation practices that require long periods of stillness can be challenging. This is where mindful movement practices like yoga or tai chi come into play. These practices combine physical movement with mindfulness, providing a dual focus that can be easier to manage than still meditation. The rhythmic, flowing movements of tai chi or the structured poses of yoga allow you to channel your energy and focus in a way that also calms the mind. They teach you how to synchronize your movements with your breath, bringing a sense of harmony and balance that can be particularly beneficial for managing ADHD symptoms.

Incorporating Mindfulness into Daily Life

Integrating mindfulness into your daily life doesn't have to involve drastic changes. It can be as simple as turning routine activities into mindful moments. For example, try turning your morning shower into a mindfulness practice. Focus on the sensations of the water hitting your skin, the sound of the water, the smell of the soap. It's about turning an everyday activity into a chance to practice focus and presence. Another practical tip is to use technology to your advantage. Set reminders on your phone for quick mindfulness breaks throughout the day or use apps that guide you through short mindfulness exercises tailored for attention span challenges.

By adapting mindfulness practices to fit the needs of the ADHD mind, you can enhance your ability to regulate emotions and manage stress, making these practices a valuable component of your daily routine. These strategies not only help in cultivating a greater sense of calm and presence but also empower you to navigate the complexities of life with ADHD with increased clarity and balance. As you integrate these practices into your life, they can become second nature, transforming not just moments of your day, but potentially the very way you experience life itself.

Strategies for Handling Anxiety and Depression in ADHD

Navigating the emotional complexities of ADHD often means dealing with more than just attention issues; it frequently involves tackling co-occurring conditions like anxiety and depression. You might wonder why these emotional challenges seem more pronounced if you're dealing with ADHD. The link between ADHD, anxiety, and depression isn't just coincidental but is deeply rooted in the neurobiological and psychosocial aspects of the disorder. ADHD can create a perpetual cycle of challenges—missed deadlines, forgotten commitments, and social mishaps—which can significantly elevate stress levels and contribute to anxiety and depression. Moreover, the same impulsivity that might cause you to leap into projects without planning can also mean that you're more susceptible to negative thought spirals, which fuel anxiety and depressive states.

Cognitive Behavioral Therapy (CBT) has shown considerable promise in helping individuals manage the symptoms of both ADHD and accompanying emotional challenges. CBT focuses on changing patterns of thinking or behavior that are behind people's difficulties, and it can be particularly effective for you if you're struggling with ADHD. This therapy helps in addressing the negative thought patterns that can lead to emotional distress, offering practical approaches to change these thoughts and reduce the feelings of anxiety and depression. For example, CBT can help modify the common ADHD-related thought pattern of "I can never do anything right" to "Everyone makes mistakes, I can learn from mine," thereby reducing feelings of worthlessness and boosting motivation. By learning to identify and alter these detrimental thought patterns, you can better manage situations that might previously have led to stress and emotional upheaval.

Discussing medication, it's vital to acknowledge that while it's not a one-size-fits-all solution, the right medication can significantly alleviate symptoms of both ADHD and its emotional comorbidities. Medications like stimulants are commonly prescribed to improve focus and reduce impulsivity in ADHD, which can indirectly help decrease anxiety and depression by enhancing your overall functionality and self-esteem. Additionally, non-stimulant medications, such as certain antidepressants, can be effective in treating both mood disorders and ADHD symptoms. However, it's crucial to navigate medication management with professional guidance, considering potential side effects and interactions. The effectiveness of medication can vary widely depending on individual differences in brain chemistry and the specific symptoms you experience, so a tailored approach, often involving some trial and error, is essential. Regular follow-ups with your healthcare provider ensure that the treatment remains aligned with your needs and adjustments are made based on your response to the medication.

Building a robust support network is another cornerstone of managing ADHD, anxiety, and depression effectively. This network should ideally include professionals who understand ADHD and its challenges, as well as peers who are navigating similar experiences, and loved ones who offer emotional and practical support. Professional support can include therapists, counselors, and medical doctors who can offer guidance, therapy, and medical interventions. Peer support, on the other hand, can provide understanding and insights from those who truly know what it's like to walk in your shoes, offering strategies that have worked for them in managing similar challenges. Moreover, loved ones can play a critical role by providing a supportive and understanding environment that helps mitigate feelings of isolation and misunderstanding often associated with ADHD and mood disorders. This multifaceted support system not only helps in providing comprehensive care but also in building a network of understanding and empathy, essential for emotional well-being.

By integrating these strategies into your life, you take proactive steps towards managing not just ADHD but also the anxiety and depression that often accompany it. Through therapy, appropriate medication management, and a strong support network, you can navigate these challenges more effectively, leading to improved mental health and a better quality of life.

The Role of Physical Exercise in Emotional Regulation

When you think about managing ADHD, physical exercise might not be the first strategy that springs to mind, but its benefits are too significant to overlook. Engaging in regular physical activity can act as a natural stimulant, enhancing mood and mitigating some of the core symptoms associated with ADHD, such as inattention, hyperactivity, and impulsivity. This stimulation arises from the increased release of endorphins, often referred to as 'feel-good' hormones, which can produce a natural high, elevating mood and creating a sense of well-being. Additionally, exercise stimulates the brain in ways similar to ADHD medication. It increases the availability of neurotransmitters like dopamine and serotonin, which are often in short supply in the ADHD brain. This biochemical boost can help improve focus, reduce feelings of anxiety, and increase energy levels, making it an essential component of emotional regulation for those with ADHD.

The type of exercise you choose can have a significant impact on its effectiveness in managing ADHD symptoms. High-intensity interval training (HIIT), for example, can be particularly beneficial. HIIT involves short bursts of intense activity followed by a brief period of rest or lower-intensity exercise. This format can be appealing if you have

ADHD, as the constant change in pace keeps the exercise engaging and prevents boredom, which is often a barrier to maintaining a regular exercise routine. The quick shifts in activity can mirror the rapid shifts in attention that characterize ADHD, providing a physical outlet for excess energy and helping to improve concentration. Team sports such as basketball, soccer, or hockey also offer unique benefits. They not only provide the physical exercise needed but also involve social interaction and require communication, cooperation, and strategy, which can help improve social skills, enhance focus, and reduce impulsivity.

Setting realistic exercise goals is crucial to developing a consistent exercise routine. The key is to set goals that are challenging yet achievable, to avoid the frustration and demotivation that can come from setting the bar too high. Start by establishing clear, measurable, and timely goals. For instance, committing to a 30-minute HIIT session twice a week or joining a community soccer team for the season are specific goals that provide a clear framework for action. It's important to track your progress and celebrate small victories along the way, which can serve as a motivational boost. Remember, consistency is more beneficial than intensity when it comes to exercise for ADHD. It's better to engage in moderate activity regularly than to push yourself too hard occasionally.

Incorporating exercise into your daily routine can be challenging, especially with the unpredictable nature of ADHD. However, there are effective strategies to make physical activity a regular part of your life. Scheduling workouts at the same time every day can help establish a routine, making it easier to remember and commit to. Packing your workout gear the night before or scheduling exercise sessions with a friend can also increase accountability and ensure you stick to your plan. Additionally, consider integrating physical activity into your daily activities. For example, a bike ride to the office or a brisk walk during lunch breaks can be an effective way to include more movement in your day. Finding activities that you genuinely enjoy is crucial. Whether it's a dance class, rock climbing, or martial arts, enjoying the activities ensures you are more likely to stick with them long term.

Creating a Personal Stress-Management Plan

Navigating the bustling currents of daily life with ADHD can often amplify stress, turning small waves into daunting tsunamis. Understanding what triggers your stress and how to manage it effectively is not just helpful; it's essential for maintaining both your mental and physical health. The first step in building a robust personal stress-management plan involves identifying your unique stressors. These are the specific situations, tasks, or people that trigger your stress response. Start by keeping a stress diary for a few weeks. In this diary, note the instances when you feel stressed, including the context and your immediate reaction. Over time, you'll begin to see patterns that reveal your primary stressors. This could be anything from last-minute deadlines and crowded places to certain social situations or even specific times of the day. Recognizing these triggers is the first step in managing them effectively.

Once you've pinpointed your stressors, the next phase is exploring various stress-reduction techniques to see which ones resonate with you. Journaling is a powerful tool that can aid in processing the events of the day and diffuse stress. It allows you to articulate thoughts and emotions on paper, which can often help in viewing them from a new perspective and reducing their intensity. Another effective technique is engaging in creative outlets like painting, music, or woodworking. These activities not only serve as a distraction from stressors but also provide a sense of accomplishment and joy, which are potent antidotes to stress. Moreover, they can be particularly beneficial for someone with ADHD as they allow for expression in a dynamic and immediate way, aligning well with the ADHD brain's need for activity and engagement.

Developing personalized strategies that integrate these techniques into your daily routine is crucial. This might look like setting aside ten minutes each evening to write in your journal, or dedicating a few hours every weekend to a creative hobby. The key is consistency and making these activities a regular part of your life, not just fallback strategies when stress peaks. Additionally, consider incorporating routines that preemptively manage stress. This might involve setting clearer boundaries at work to prevent last-minute pressures, or organizing social interactions in environments that feel safe and comfortable for you, minimizing social stress.

Regularly monitoring and adjusting your stress-management plan is vital to its success. This means periodically reviewing the effectiveness of your strategies and being open to making changes as needed. Perhaps a certain technique isn't working as well as you hoped, or a new stressor has entered your life. Adjusting your plan to accommodate these changes ensures that it remains relevant and effective. This ongoing process not only helps in managing current stress but also in developing resilience against future stressors.

As this chapter wraps up, remember that managing stress is not about eliminating it completely but about understanding and mitigating its impact on your life. By identifying your stress triggers, experimenting with and implementing effective stress-reduction techniques, and regularly updating your approach, you can maintain a healthier, more balanced life. This proactive approach to stress management is especially crucial in navigating the complexities of life with

ADHD, where the waves can seem relentless. With your personalized plan in hand, you're better equipped to steer through these waters, prepared for both the squalls and the calms.

As we close this exploration of stress management, we pave the way to the next chapter where we delve into the intricacies of organizational skills for home and work. Here, we'll explore practical strategies to transform potential chaos into structured harmony, enhancing both personal efficiency and peace of mind.

CHAPTER 7: ORGANIZATIONAL SKILLS FOR HOME AND WORK

Imagine walking into a room where every item has a place, the surfaces are clear, and each drawer holds only what you need, nothing more, nothing less. This might sound like a distant dream, especially when the daily reality often involves searching for keys under piles of unsorted mail or navigating through cluttered spaces just to find the remote. For adults with ADHD, the challenge of keeping spaces organized can often feel like an uphill battle, with the chaos outside often mirroring the whirlwind of thoughts inside. However, the impact of a decluttered and well-organized environment on your mental clarity and productivity can be profound. This chapter is designed to guide you through transforming cluttered chaos into streamlined simplicity, enhancing both your personal and professional life.

Decluttering Your Space: ADHD-Friendly Approaches

The Importance of a Decluttered Space

Clutter is not just a physical nuisance; it can also be a significant cognitive burden for anyone, particularly so if you're navigating the complexities of ADHD. An environment filled with unnecessary items can lead to sensory overload, exacerbating feelings of stress and making it difficult to focus. Each unsorted stack of papers or jumbled drawer competes for your attention, pulling it away from tasks that actually need it. By decluttering, you not only clear your physical space but also free up mental space, which can lead to improved concentration and reduced anxiety. The process involves evaluating what truly needs to be in your environment and removing the extraneous, not just once but as a maintained habit. This ongoing practice helps in minimizing distractions, making it easier to engage deeply and meaningfully with your work and home life.

Step-by-Step Decluttering Guide

Embarking on decluttering can seem daunting, especially when you're unsure where to begin. A step-by-step approach can turn this seemingly insurmountable task into a series of manageable, achievable steps. Start with one small area—this could be a desk drawer or a single shelf—rather than tackling an entire room at once. Remove everything from the space so you can see it clearly and sort items into categories: keep, throw away, donate, or relocate. Be ruthless in your assessment; if an item hasn't been used in over a year or it doesn't bring significant value or joy into your life, it's likely clutter. Once you've pared down the contents, consider the best way to organize what remains. Use organizers, trays, or dividers to give everything a designated place. This not only makes items easier to find but also simplifies the process of returning them to their spots, maintaining the order you've created.

Maintaining a Minimalist Mindset

Adopting a minimalist mindset goes beyond the initial act of decluttering; it's about embracing simplicity in your ongoing interactions with your surroundings. This mindset encourages thoughtful acquisition and retention of items, questioning the utility and necessity of each object in your space. Start by establishing rules for new acquisitions, such as 'one in, one out,' where a new item can only enter your space if another leaves. Regularly review and clear out your spaces to avoid the slow creep of clutter. This proactive approach not only keeps your environment under control but also cultivates a sense of peace and order, making daily life smoother and more enjoyable.

Organizational Tools and Resources

To support your organizational efforts, a variety of tools and resources are available that can significantly enhance your ability to maintain an orderly environment. Label makers, for instance, can be indispensable in clearly identifying contents of boxes, drawers, and folders, reducing the time spent searching for items. Storage solutions like clear bins and baskets allow you to see contents at a glance, while modular shelving units can be adapted to fit your changing needs. For paper management, consider a scanner to digitize important documents, reducing physical clutter and making them easier to locate electronically. Investing in these tools not only aids in maintaining organization but also makes the process more efficient and less cumbersome, aligning well with the ADHD brain's preference for streamlined, straightforward systems.

By implementing these strategies, you create an environment that supports rather than hinders your daily functioning. A decluttered space not only enhances focus and productivity but also contributes to a calmer, more controlled mindset, allowing you to navigate both home and work life with greater ease and efficiency. As we continue to explore organizational skills in the following sections, remember that the foundation of a well-organized life is not just about placing things neatly—it's about creating a space that reflects and supports your best self.

The Digital Declutter: Managing Online Distractions

In today's hyper-connected world, the constant barrage of notifications, emails, and endless streams of social media updates can significantly hinder your ability to focus, particularly when dealing with ADHD. The digital environment, much like a physical one, can become cluttered with unnecessary distractions that fragment your attention and drain your mental energy. Recognizing and minimizing this digital clutter is crucial for maintaining productivity and reducing stress, especially for those who might find their attention easily hijacked by the ping of a new email or the buzz of a smartphone notification.

Digital clutter encompasses all those files, apps, notifications, and emails that are not essential but occupy space, both physically on your devices and mentally in your mind. To identify digital clutter, start by assessing your digital usage. Notice which apps you use frequently and which ones you haven't opened in months. Look at your desktop and download folders; are they filled with old documents and images you no longer need? Do your email inboxes contain newsletters you never read or old messages that simply gather digital dust? This process of identification is the first step towards a cleaner, more organized digital life. Once you pinpoint the sources of digital clutter, the path to reducing it becomes clearer and more navigable.

Reducing digital distractions can significantly enhance your focus and productivity. One effective strategy is the use of app blockers or features that limit screen time. Tools like Freedom or Cold Turkey allow you to block distracting websites or apps during designated times, helping you to maintain focus on priority tasks. Consider implementing scheduled digital detoxes—designated times when you disconnect from all digital devices. This could be during meals, the first hour after waking up, or late in the evening before bed. These detox periods can help reduce dependence on digital stimuli and improve your ability to concentrate on tasks without interruptions. Additionally, adjusting notification settings plays a critical role in managing digital distractions. Customize your device settings to allow only essential notifications; this means turning off pop-ups for social media, promotional emails, and other non-essential communications. By controlling what alerts you receive and when you can significantly decrease the cognitive load placed on you by continual interruptions.

Organizing digital files and information is also crucial in managing digital clutter. Start with your email since it's often the biggest source of digital overload. Create folders or labels to categorize emails effectively. Use filters to automatically direct incoming emails to these folders, which can help keep your inbox manageable. Unsubscribe from newsletters or promotions you no longer find useful. For digital files, create a clear, hierarchical folder structure on your computer. Regularly archive old files and delete those you no longer need. Cloud storage services can be useful for keeping important documents accessible without using physical storage space on your device. Implementing a regular review and clean-up schedule for your digital files can prevent them from becoming overwhelming and ensure that you can always find what you need, when you need it, without unnecessary stress or frustration.

Setting boundaries with technology is vital for maintaining mental clarity and reducing stress. Establish clear rules for how and when you engage with digital devices. This might involve having tech-free zones in your home, such as the bedroom or dining area, where digital devices are not allowed, or setting specific times when you check emails or social media. These boundaries help to create spaces where you can relax and unwind without the constant demand for your attention that digital devices often impose. They also encourage healthier habits around technology use, making it easier to disconnect and engage in more fulfilling offline activities, ultimately improving your overall well-being and productivity.

By taking these steps towards decluttering your digital life, you not only make space on your devices but also free up your mental landscape, allowing for deeper focus and greater peace of mind. This cleaner, more organized digital environment supports your efforts in managing ADHD, making it easier to stay on task and reduce the feelings of being overwhelmed that too often accompany this condition. As you continue to implement these strategies, you'll likely find that your days are not only more productive but also more satisfying, with a balanced approach to technology that supports your goals rather than detracts from them.

Organizing Tasks: Visual Systems for the ADHD Brain

In the bustling theater of your daily life, where numerous tasks clamor for attention like eager actors on a stage, maintaining order and focus can often feel overwhelming. For individuals with ADHD, this challenge is intensified by a brain wiring that juggles multiple thoughts and stimuli at once, often dropping them in the process. Visual task management systems, such as Kanban boards, offer a dynamic solution by transforming abstract tasks into tangible, visual elements that are easier to manage and track. These systems leverage the ADHD brain's inherent preference for visual processing over textual or auditory information, providing a clear, visual overview of tasks that helps in prioritizing and organizing your activities effectively.

Kanban boards, originally developed as a scheduling system to improve manufacturing efficiency, are remarkably effective for personal productivity as well. They work by mapping out tasks on cards or digital blocks, which are then placed in columns that represent different stages of the process, typically labeled as 'To Do,' 'Doing,' and 'Done.' This setup not only gives you a visual snapshot of your current workload and progress but also simplifies the process of managing multiple tasks. By physically moving a task from one column to the next, you gain a tangible sense of progression, which can be highly motivating. Moreover, this movement provides a physical action that can help in maintaining focus, a frequent challenge for those with ADHD. The clarity and structure imposed by this system reduce the cognitive load of remembering and organizing tasks, allowing you to direct more mental energy towards actually completing them.

Visual task management systems thrive on customization, and creating a system tailored to your specific needs can significantly enhance its effectiveness. Start by identifying the categories that best reflect your workflow. While the basic 'To Do,' 'Doing,' and 'Done' columns work well, you might find it helpful to add additional categories like 'Waiting for Feedback,' 'Urgent,' or 'Ideas.' Customize your board to reflect your personal or professional life's unique stages and requirements. If you're managing projects that involve multiple steps or teams, consider a more complex setup with columns for each phase of the project or each team's responsibilities. The flexibility to mold the system to fit your tasks and responsibilities is one of its greatest strengths, making it an invaluable tool for anyone looking to bring order to the chaos of their daily tasks.

Using Color Coding

The human brain is naturally drawn to colors; they can influence mood, convey information, and attract attention. In the context of visual task management, color coding serves as an efficient way to categorize and prioritize tasks, making the system even more intuitive and accessible. By assigning specific colors to different types of tasks, levels of urgency, or project phases, you can gain an instant understanding of your workload's nature and priorities just by glancing at your board. For instance, using red for urgent tasks, blue for ongoing projects, and green for completed tasks not only brightens up your task board but also allows you to quickly assess your progress and adjust your focus accordingly.

To implement color coding effectively, select a palette that is visually distinct and aligns with your personal preferences or the emotional tone of the tasks. Simplicity is key—too many colors can become confusing and counterproductive. Stick to a limited range of colors and consistently apply them across your tasks. You can also use color coding in conjunction with other organizational tools like labels or tags to provide additional layers of information. For example, alongside color coding for urgency, you might use labels to indicate task duration or the required energy level, providing a comprehensive at-a-glance overview of your tasks.

Incorporating Technology

In our digital age, technology offers powerful tools that can enhance and complement traditional visual task management systems. Digital Kanban apps like Trello, Asana, or Monday.com take the principles of Kanban boards and translate them into versatile, feature-rich digital platforms. These tools offer the benefits of traditional Kanban boards, such as visual task management and customizable columns, along with added features like cloud syncing, collaboration tools, and automated reminders. For individuals with ADHD, these digital systems can be particularly beneficial, providing the ability to manage tasks from any device, share and collaborate on boards with team members or family, and integrate with other digital tools like calendars or email.

When integrating technology into your visual task management system, consider how different tools can interact to create a seamless workflow. For instance, most digital Kanban tools allow you to attach files directly to tasks, link tasks to specific emails, or set up integrations with calendar apps to automatically schedule time for task completion. These integrations not only save time but also centralize your organizational system, reducing the need to switch between different apps and potentially lose focus. As you explore various technological options, prioritize tools that sync across all your devices, ensuring you can access and update your task management system whether you're at home, at work, or on the go.

By leveraging visual task management systems, color coding, and technology, you create a robust framework that harnesses your visual processing strengths. This approach not only enhances your organizational skills but also aligns with the natural inclinations of the ADHD brain, making it easier to maintain focus, prioritize tasks, and ultimately drive productivity in both your personal and professional life.

Long-Term Planning When You're Wired for the Now

Long-term planning often feels like trying to read a map in the fog when you're managing ADHD. The immediate demands—those urgent "right now" tasks—often overshadow goals that seem distant on the horizon. This focus on the immediate is a common trait for individuals with ADHD, making the concept of planning weeks, months, or even years into the future daunting and sometimes disorienting. Yet, developing the skill to look beyond the immediate can transform fleeting success into sustained achievement and satisfaction. It's about expanding your temporal view, recognizing that today's actions lay the groundwork for tomorrow's outcomes.

Setting realistic, achievable long-term goals is a cornerstone of effective planning. These goals should resonate with your personal values and aspirations, transforming them from distant duties into meaningful milestones. Begin by articulating what you truly value—be it career advancement, personal growth, relationship stability, or financial security. These values become the compass that guides your goal-setting process. When setting goals, ensure they are SMART: Specific, Measurable, Achievable, Relevant, and Time-bound. For instance, rather than a vague goal like "get better at finances," a SMART goal would be "save $5,000 for an emergency fund within two years by setting aside $210 each month." This clarity not only provides a direct pathway towards your goal but also embeds it within a realistic timeframe, enhancing your commitment and the likelihood of success.

Breaking down these long-term goals into short-term actions and milestones is crucial, especially when daily distractions can easily derail your focus. This breakdown acts like a bridge, turning the distant vision into approachable steps. Start by outlining the major milestones needed to achieve your goal. For a goal like saving for an emergency fund, milestones might include saving the first $1,000, setting up a dedicated savings account, or consulting a financial advisor. Each milestone should have associated actions, such as reviewing monthly expenses to find savings opportunities or setting up automatic bank transfers. These actions should fit comfortably into your daily or weekly routines, making them manageable rather than overwhelming. By regularly achieving small successes, you maintain momentum and reinforce your commitment to the larger goal, gradually building a track record of accomplishments that support your ultimate objectives.

The importance of regularly reviewing and adjusting your goals cannot be overstated. Life's only constant is change, and your planning needs to adapt to reflect new information, shifting priorities, or unexpected obstacles. Set periodic reviews—monthly, quarterly, or annually—to assess your progress and make necessary adjustments. These reviews are opportunities to celebrate successes, learn from setbacks, and refine your strategies to ensure they remain aligned with your changing circumstances and insights. If a particular approach isn't working, don't hesitate to experiment with new strategies or seek advice to enhance your planning effectiveness. This flexible, responsive approach ensures that your planning process remains dynamic and relevant, accurately reflecting your current reality and future aspirations.

As you integrate these strategies into your life, remember that long-term planning is not just about reaching a destination. It's about crafting a journey that is meaningful and aligned with who you are and who you aspire to be. Each step, each decision, and each adjustment is part of a larger narrative of personal growth and achievement. This chapter has equipped you with the tools to expand your planning horizon, break down daunting goals into achievable steps, and adapt your strategies to meet the evolving landscape of your life.

As we close this chapter on organizational skills, we prepare to explore the next crucial aspect of managing ADHD: Health, Diet, and Lifestyle. This upcoming chapter will delve into how optimizing your physical health through diet, exercise, and lifestyle choices can significantly impact your ADHD management, enhancing both your mental and physical well-being. These foundational elements of health are not just supportive of your ADHD management strategies; they are essential to your overall quality of life, providing the physical and mental energy to pursue your goals and enjoy your achievements.

CHAPTER 8: HEALTH, DIET, AND LIFESTYLE

Picture this: You're at the starting line of a race, poised and ready. Your body is a race car, and just like high-performance vehicles require the right fuel to run efficiently, your body, especially when managing ADHD, demands the right nutritional inputs to perform at its best. In this chapter, we'll delve into how the foods you eat, the supplements you might consider, and even your hydration levels play pivotal roles in either fueling or frustrating your ADHD symptoms. As we navigate these nutritional pathways, think of yourself as both the driver and the mechanic of your own body, ensuring it gets what it needs to race smoothly and efficiently through the twists and turns of daily life with ADHD.

Nutrition and ADHD: Foods That Help and Hinder

Impact of Diet on ADHD Symptoms

The link between diet and ADHD symptoms is more significant than many realize. Certain foods can exacerbate ADHD symptoms, while others can help alleviate them, acting almost like natural medication. For instance, high-sugar foods, artificial additives, and common allergens such as gluten or dairy are often reported to increase hyperactivity, impulsiveness, and distractibility among those with ADHD. Conversely, a diet rich in protein, complex carbohydrates, and omega-3 fatty acids has been shown to improve focus, stabilize mood, and increase overall cognitive function. This is because proteins and complex carbs help in the slow and steady release of glucose, your brain's primary source of fuel, while omega-3s are vital for brain function and development. Think of your diet as a dial controlling the volume of your symptoms; with the right foods, you can turn down the distractions and enhance your focus.

ADHD-Friendly Diet Tips

Creating an ADHD-friendly diet starts with incorporating foods that are high in protein, fiber, and healthy fats. Begin your day with a protein-rich breakfast to kickstart your brain and keep you satiated and focused throughout the morning. Options like eggs, Greek yogurt, or a smoothie with protein powder, spinach, and a small handful of berries can be excellent choices. Throughout the day, integrate whole grains, fruits, vegetables, and lean proteins into your meals and snacks.

These foods help maintain stable blood sugar levels and provide essential nutrients that your brain needs to function optimally. Also, consider preparing meals ahead of time. ADHD can sometimes make meal planning and cooking feel overwhelming, so having ready-to-eat healthy options on hand can prevent you from reaching for less nutritious, impulse-driven snacks.

The Role of Hydration

Hydration plays a crucial, yet often overlooked, role in managing ADHD symptoms. Dehydration can cause fatigue, irritability, and distractibility—all familiar foes for those with ADHD. Water is essential not just for physical health but also for cognitive function, as it facilitates the flow of nutrients to your brain and helps eliminate toxins. Aim to drink at least eight 8-ounce glasses of water a day, more if you consume diuretics like caffeine, which can increase fluid loss. Keeping a water bottle at your desk or setting reminders on your phone can help ensure you meet your daily hydration goals. Remember, your brain is about 75% water; keeping it hydrated is akin to keeping your car's engine well-oiled.

Supplements and ADHD

While a balanced diet is the cornerstone of good health, certain supplements may be beneficial in managing ADHD symptoms, particularly if dietary intake alone falls short. Omega-3 fatty acids, for instance, are critical for brain health. Studies suggest that supplements containing EPA and DHA, types of omega-3s found in fish oil, can improve attention, cognitive function, and behavior in individuals with ADHD. Magnesium, often deficient in the typical Western diet, plays a role in calming the nervous system and is linked to improved sleep and reduced hyperactivity. Zinc, too, is important, as it helps regulate dopamine, a neurotransmitter that is often out of balance in ADHD. Before starting any supplement regimen, however, it's important to consult with a healthcare provider, as supplements can interact with medications and other nutrients.

By understanding and adjusting your diet and hydration, and thoughtfully considering supplements, you're not just feeding your body; you're making strategic choices that support your brain's unique wiring. This thoughtful approach to nutrition can significantly enhance your ability to manage your symptoms and improve your overall quality of life with ADHD.

The Impact of Sleep on ADHD Symptoms

Understanding the intricate dance between sleep and ADHD is crucial for anyone grappling with this condition. Sleep issues are not just a minor inconvenience; they can exacerbate ADHD symptoms, creating a vicious cycle where sleeplessness heightens ADHD challenges, which in turn can lead to even worse sleep. Many adults with ADHD struggle with what's known as "delayed sleep phase syndrome," where their internal clock pushes them toward later sleep and wake times, making conventional schedules challenging. Additionally, the restless mind associated with ADHD often finds it hard to shut down at night, leading to prolonged periods of wakefulness that hinder the ability to fall asleep.

This bidirectional relationship means that managing sleep is not just about getting enough hours, but about enhancing the quality of sleep to ensure that the brain functions optimally. Implementing structured sleep hygiene practices can make a significant difference.

Begin by establishing a consistent bedtime routine that cues your body for sleep. This might involve winding down activities an hour before bed, engaging in a relaxing activity like reading (preferably not on a screen), or practicing relaxation exercises such as deep breathing or progressive muscle relaxation to calm the mind and reduce hyper-arousal. It's also helpful to synchronize your sleep schedule to your natural circadian rhythms as much as possible. If you find that your natural sleep time is later, try to structure your day so that you can wake up later in the morning, aligning your sleep pattern with your body's internal clock rather than fighting against it.

The management of stimulant medications is another critical factor in the sleep-ADHD equation. Stimulants, often prescribed to manage ADHD symptoms, can significantly disrupt sleep patterns if not properly timed. The key is to fine-tune the timing and dosage in consultation with your healthcare provider. For some, taking medication earlier in the day can help minimize its impact on sleep, while others might need to adjust the dosage or switch to a different medication altogether. Extended-release formulas can also alter sleep patterns differently than immediate-release forms, so discussing these options with a doctor who understands the nuances of ADHD medications can be transformative in managing both wakefulness and sleep.

Creating a restful sleeping environment also plays a pivotal role in combating sleep issues. This begins with making your bedroom a sanctuary for sleep. Consider the sensory environment of your sleep space: is it conducive to relaxation? Many with ADHD are sensitive to sensory inputs, so it's essential to minimize any disruptive factors. Use blackout curtains to darken the room, as even minimal light can disturb the sleep cycle. If noise is an issue, white noise machines or earplugs can be beneficial. The temperature of the room should be comfortably cool, as overheating can disrupt sleep. Moreover, investing in a good quality mattress and pillows can provide the physical comfort necessary for a good night's rest, supporting your body's needs and alleviating discomfort that might keep you awake.

By addressing these aspects of sleep—understanding its impact on ADHD, implementing robust sleep hygiene practices, managing medications appropriately, and creating a conducive sleep environment—you equip yourself with the tools not just for better sleep, but for better management of ADHD symptoms. Improved sleep can lead to enhanced daily functioning, mood stability, and overall life quality, turning what often feels like a nightly struggle into an opportunity for healing and restoration.

Exercise Routines That Boost Focus and Reduce Impulsivity

Although we have already briefly touched on the role physical exercise plays, this section dives into finding the right type of exercise routines that work for you and your ADHD symptoms.

Finding the right type of exercise to manage ADHD symptoms can be akin to custom-fitting a key to a lock. Specific activities, particularly those demanding a blend of physical exertion, mental engagement, and discipline, can dramatically enhance focus and curb impulsivity. Martial arts and team sports stand out as two prime examples. Martial arts, such as karate, judo, or tai chi, require a high level of mental discipline and focus, making them more than just physical activities. They are structured in ways that demand attention to detail, constant mental engagement, and adherence to routines, all of which provide the brain with a full workout. The repetitive nature of martial arts drills, combined with the strategic thinking involved in mastering moves, helps in cultivating a sense of inner calm and focus. This discipline spills over into daily life, aiding in better impulse control and attention management.

Team sports like soccer, basketball, or hockey also offer unique benefits. They are dynamic and fast-paced, which keeps the brain engaged and alert, helping to burn off excess energy and reduce impulsivity. The social aspect of team sports cannot be overstated; they require communication, cooperation, and strategy, which are all skills that can sometimes be challenging for those with ADHD. Engaging in these sports encourages the development of these skills in a fun and supportive environment. Moreover, the structured nature of team sports, with set practice times and game schedules, provides a routine that can help bring regularity and predictability to your week, aiding in overall time management and planning.

Building a consistent exercise routine is crucial, yet it can be daunting if you feel like your daily schedule is already packed or unpredictable. The key to success is integration rather than addition; find ways to incorporate physical activity into your existing schedule. If mornings are hectic, consider a brief workout during lunch or after work. Even 15 to 20 minutes can be beneficial. Start with activities you enjoy, as enjoyment increases the likelihood of sticking with them. Setting small, achievable goals, such as attending a martial arts class twice a week or joining a weekend basketball league, provides clear targets and helps build momentum. Gradually increase the frequency and intensity of workouts as your stamina and schedule allow. Remember, consistency leads to habits, and habits form the backbone of effective ADHD management.

Physical activity plays a pivotal role in emotional regulation and stress management. Exercise induces the release of endorphins, often referred to as feel-good hormones, which can elevate mood and create feelings of well-being. Regular physical activity also helps in regulating the sleep cycle and reducing anxiety, both of which can be problematic for individuals with ADHD. Engaging in regular, vigorous exercise such as martial arts or participating in team sports provides an outlet for pent-up energy and helps reduce tension. The focus required for these activities also offers a mental break from daily stressors, allowing you to disconnect from worries and immerse yourself in the moment, providing a restorative mental pause that can reduce overall stress levels.

Despite the clear benefits, starting and maintaining a regular exercise routine can be challenging. Common barriers include lack of time, perceived boredom with exercise, or feelings of self-consciousness, especially if you're starting a new activity. Overcoming these obstacles starts with a shift in perspective; view exercise as a non-negotiable part of your health care, not just an optional add-on. To combat boredom, vary your activities; mix team sports with individual exercises like swimming or cycling, or martial arts with gym workouts. Address time constraints by combining physical activity with social or family time. For instance, biking with friends or playing sports with family can enhance relationships while also providing the needed physical activity. For those feeling self-conscious, remember that everyone starts somewhere, and most people are too focused on their workouts to notice others. Alternatively, starting with home workouts or classes specifically designed for beginners can ease you into the exercise world more gently.

The Role of Routine in an ADHD Life

Routines often get a bad rap for being the dull drumbeat to the vibrant spontaneity of life. Yet, when you're navigating the world with ADHD, establishing routines can be like setting GPS coordinates on a chaotic journey, guiding you towards efficiency and reducing the stress of constant decision-making. Think of routines not as constraints but as frameworks that free you to focus your energy and creativity on what truly matters. For individuals with ADHD, routines can significantly reduce decision fatigue—a real concern given the daily barrage of choices everyone faces. By automating some of these decisions, routines help conserve your mental bandwidth for tasks that require active thinking and creativity, enhancing overall productivity and reducing the feeling of being overwhelmed.

Creating effective routines that resonate with the ADHD brain involves understanding and aligning with your natural rhythms and preferences. Start by identifying the times of day when you feel most energetic and attentive. Are you a morning person, or do you find your stride in the evening? Use this insight to schedule tasks that require high concentration during these peak periods. Incorporate time buffers around tasks to accommodate the unexpected distractions or hyperfocus episodes that are common with ADHD. For daily routines, consider implementing solid start and end rituals. Morning routines might include a brief planning session where you outline your key tasks for the day, coupled with a consistent wake-up time and a simple breakfast routine. Evening routines could involve a wind-down period with activities that promote relaxation, such as reading or light stretching, signaling to your brain that it's time to shift gears towards rest.

Flexibility within structure is crucial when setting routines for ADHD. The unpredictable nature of ADHD symptoms means some days will inevitably go off-script. Instead of rigidly adhering to a failed plan, adaptability should be built into your routines. This could mean having a contingency plan for when tasks take longer than expected or shifting less critical tasks to another day. It's also beneficial to regularly review and adjust your routines. What works one month might not be effective the next as your life circumstances and priorities change. Regular reviews allow you to tweak your routines, ensuring they continue to serve your needs effectively.

Tools and strategies for maintaining routines are vital in ensuring they stick. Visual schedules can be particularly effective. These might take the form of large wall planners or digital calendars that provide a clear overview of your day, week, or month. These visual cues act as constant reminders of what needs to be done, reducing the chance of forgetting important tasks. Additionally, using reminder systems can bolster your routines. Set alarms or notifications for time-sensitive tasks or transitions between activities. Apps like Google Calendar or Todoist can be set to remind you of upcoming tasks, providing nudges when it's time to switch gears. For those who find too many notifications overwhelming, consider a minimalist approach by setting only the most critical reminders.

Incorporating these elements into your life doesn't just help manage ADHD; it creates a framework that enhances your ability to navigate daily challenges more smoothly and effectively. Routines provide a predictable rhythm that can reduce anxiety and improve time management, making daily life less about firefighting and more about thriving. As you refine these routines, they become less like chains and more like the tracks that guide a train towards its destination—efficiently and on time.

As we wrap up this exploration of the pivotal role routines play in managing ADHD, remember that the goal is to create a flexible structure that supports and enhances your daily functioning. By building and maintaining effective routines, you equip yourself to handle the complexities of ADHD with greater ease and confidence, paving the way for improved productivity and stability. Transitioning from the detailed strategies discussed here, the next chapter will focus on leveraging ADHD in the workplace, where we'll explore how to apply your unique skills and adapt strategies to thrive professionally. This shift from personal routines to professional success highlights the comprehensive approach needed to manage ADHD effectively across all areas of life.

CHAPTER 9: LEVERAGING ADHD IN THE WORKPLACE

I magine stepping into a workspace that not only accepts but applauds the very traits that others might label as distractions. In the right environment, what is often seen as a hurdle can become your greatest asset. This chapter is dedicated to transforming how you view ADHD in the context of your professional life. It's about aligning your unique abilities with career paths that not only accommodate but celebrate your distinctive way of thinking and operating. Here, we delve into identifying ADHD-friendly careers and work environments that encourage you to thrive, not despite, but because of your ADHD.

Identifying ADHD-Friendly Careers and Work Environments

Highlighting Strengths

The narrative often surrounding ADHD focuses on the obstacles it might create. However, the tide is turning, with a growing recognition of the unique strengths brought to the table by individuals with ADHD. Traits such as hyperfocus, creativity, resilience, and the ability to think outside the box are highly prized in many modern workplaces. These qualities can make you an invaluable asset in fields that thrive on innovation and quick thinking. Careers in creative industries like advertising, digital media, and product development, or roles that require problem-solving and adaptability, such as IT, entrepreneurship, and emergency services, can be particularly rewarding. In these dynamic settings, your ability to generate novel ideas and swiftly adapt to changing circumstances can set you apart from the crowd. It's about flipping the script—where others see inattention, you can demonstrate boundless creativity; where some perceive impulsivity, you can highlight your capacity for rapid decision-making.

ADHD-Friendly Work Environments

An ADHD-friendly work environment is one that not only accommodates but actively supports the way your brain functions. Such workplaces are characterized by flexibility, understanding, and support. Flexibility might manifest in adjustable work hours or the ability to work remotely, catering to varying productivity patterns and helping you work during your peak focus times. Engaging tasks are crucial—jobs that provide variety and learning opportunities can keep you stimulated and prevent boredom, which is often kryptonite for someone with ADHD. Supportive management plays a critical role; this includes supervisors who understand ADHD and are committed to making necessary adjustments, such as clear and structured expectations, regular feedback, and recognition of your successes. These elements create an environment where you can excel, turning potential ADHD-induced challenges into professional strengths.

Career Path Exploration

Venturing into the professional world with ADHD involves more than just understanding your symptoms; it requires a deep dive into your passions and strengths. Start by assessing what you love doing—consider projects or tasks, both at work and outside, that ignite your enthusiasm and where time seems to fly. Utilize career counseling services or ADHD coaching to help uncover potential career paths that align with your interests and strengths. Tools like personality assessments and career aptitude tests can offer insights into job roles that might suit your unique skill set. Remember, the goal is to find a career that not only accommodates your ADHD but one where your natural talents and inclinations can shine.

Personal Success Stories

To inspire and guide you, consider the stories of those who have navigated similar paths. Take, for example, the story of a graphic designer who turned his hyperfocus to his advantage, creating award-winning designs under tight deadlines, or the entrepreneur with ADHD whose ability to think differently helped her develop a revolutionary tech startup. These stories not only serve as proof of what's possible but also provide practical insights into navigating the workplace with ADHD. They highlight strategies such as the use of technology to manage tasks, the importance of a supportive network, and personal adjustments like tailored work schedules that align with one's productivity peaks.

Interactive Element: Reflective Journaling Prompt

Reflect on Your Ideal Work Environment

Take a moment to reflect on what your ideal ADHD-friendly work environment would look like. Consider the kind of tasks that would keep you engaged, the type of management style that you find supportive, and the accommodations that would help you perform at your best. Write down these reflections and use them as a guide in your current job or in discussions with potential employers. This exercise not only clarifies what conditions help you thrive but also empowers you to seek or create work environments that align with your needs.

Strategies for Effective Meetings and Presentations

When it comes to navigating the corporate seas, meetings and presentations can often seem like daunting waves for someone with ADHD. The key to not only surviving but excelling in these situations lies in adapting conventional preparation techniques to fit your unique cognitive style. Tailoring these strategies ensures you're not just ready but confident when stepping into the meeting room or presenting in front of an audience. Start by breaking down the preparation process into smaller, manageable segments. If you have a presentation, begin by drafting an outline well in advance. This outline acts as your roadmap, highlighting key points and helping maintain your train of thought during the presentation. For meetings, prepare by reviewing the agenda and noting down any questions or comments you might have about each item. This preparation not only aids in keeping you engaged during the meeting but also ensures you contribute meaningfully.

Transitioning into the actual presentation, leverage your natural ADHD strengths such as dynamic energy and creativity. Presentations that tell a story or include a narrative element are not only more engaging but also easier for you to deliver because they harness your innate storytelling abilities. Utilize visuals like slides or props to maintain audience interest and help anchor your own focus. Keeping your presentation lively with changes in tone, gestures, and even incorporating audience interaction can help maintain your engagement levels and prevent your mind from wandering. These techniques not only captivate your audience but also play to your strengths, allowing you to deliver powerful and memorable presentations.

Maintaining attention during meetings can be particularly challenging. The key here is active participation. Take detailed notes, which helps in retaining information and maintaining focus. If note-taking is challenging, consider using a digital recorder or a note-taking app that can transcribe discussions in real-time, allowing you to revisit them later. Asking questions not only clarifies points you might have missed but also demonstrates your engagement and interest. If you find your attention waning, it can be helpful to have a discreet physical activity, such as a stress ball or a fidget spinner, which can aid in maintaining focus without distracting others.

Finally, the pursuit of excellence in meetings and presentations is a continuous journey. Proactively seek feedback from colleagues and supervisors after your presentations or contributions in meetings. This feedback is invaluable as it provides perspectives outside your own, highlighting areas of strength and aspects needing improvement. Embrace this feedback with an open mind and use it as a foundation for continual improvement. Regularly reflect on your own performances as well, identifying patterns in what works and what doesn't, and adjust your strategies accordingly. This proactive approach not only enhances your skills but also boosts your confidence, making each meeting and presentation better than the last.

By incorporating these tailored strategies into your professional routine, you transform potential stumbling blocks into stepping stones for success, turning every meeting and presentation into an opportunity to showcase your unique abilities and professional value.

Networking and Career Growth with ADHD

Navigating the professional landscape with ADHD often means adapting typical career advancement strategies to fit your unique cognitive and social patterns. Effective networking, for instance, can sometimes feel daunting due to potential distractions or social anxiety that might accompany ADHD. However, by leveraging your innate abilities for genuine connection and embracing platforms that align with your strengths, you can make networking a powerful tool for career growth. Let's explore ADHD-friendly networking strategies that capitalize on shared interests and authentic communication, making the process of building professional relationships both enjoyable and productive.

Networking for you isn't just about exchanging business cards or making LinkedIn connections; it's about forming meaningful relationships based on shared interests and genuine interactions. This approach plays directly to your strengths. Your ability to be enthusiastic and passionate about subjects that interest you can be magnetic, drawing others to you naturally. Start by identifying networking events that align with your interests or are relevant to your industry. These could be informal meet-ups, workshops, or seminars that focus on areas you are passionate about. Once there, use your natural curiosity to engage in conversations. Ask questions, listen actively, and share your thoughts. This genuine interest can make conversations more engaging and memorable, helping you form connections that are based on true mutual interests rather than just superficial exchanges.

Moreover, the dynamic nature of social media presents both opportunities and challenges for networking when you have ADHD. Platforms like Twitter, LinkedIn, and industry-specific online forums can be excellent tools for connecting with peers, industry leaders, and potential mentors. They allow you to engage with networking opportunities from the comfort of your home, which can sometimes be less intimidating than face-to-face interactions. To effectively leverage these platforms, focus on creating content that reflects your professional interests and insights. Share articles, write posts, or comment on discussions that align with your areas of expertise or passion. This not only helps in building your professional brand but also attracts connections who share your interests. However, it's crucial to manage potential distractions that come with social media. Use tools like website blockers to limit the time spent on social media or set specific times during the day for social media activities, ensuring it remains a tool for networking rather than a source of procrastination.

Finding mentors who understand the nuances of ADHD can significantly impact your professional development. A mentor who gets how your brain operates can offer more than just career guidance; they can provide strategies for handling workplace challenges that are specific to ADHD, such as organization, time management, and maintaining focus. To find such mentors, look within your existing professional network or consider reaching out to ADHD advocacy groups where professionals gather. When you find a potential mentor, be open about your ADHD and how it affects your professional life. This transparency allows them to provide tailored advice and support that genuinely addresses your needs. Regular meetings with your mentor can offer a steady source of guidance, accountability, and encouragement, which can be invaluable in navigating your career path.

Continuous learning and development are crucial in maintaining career growth, especially in today's fast-paced professional environment. However, traditional learning environments or resources may not always be the best fit for your learning style. Seek out learning opportunities that are interactive and offer practical, real-world applications, as these are more likely to hold your attention and result in meaningful learning. Online courses that offer short, engaging modules or hands-on workshops in your local community can be particularly effective. Additionally, consider resources that are specifically designed for individuals with ADHD. These might include courses that offer strategies for improving focus and productivity or forums where professionals with ADHD share tips and experiences. Engaging with these resources not only helps you stay updated with your industry's trends and skills but also provides strategies for managing your ADHD in the professional world.

By embracing these ADHD-friendly networking and learning strategies, you position yourself not just to succeed but to excel in your career. Your approach to building relationships based on genuine interests and managing your professional development with your unique needs in mind isn't just about career growth. It's about crafting a professional life that is as vibrant and dynamic as you are, leveraging your ADHD traits as assets that propel you forward in your career journey.

Turning Hyperfocus into a Professional Superpower

Hyperfocus, often a hallmark of ADHD, can be likened to a laser beam—intensely powerful and focused, yet challenging to control. When harnessed correctly, it can elevate your work performance to exceptional levels, turning intricate projects into masterpieces of productivity. The key lies in channeling this unique ability towards tasks and projects that not only capture your interest but also align with your professional goals. By strategically steering your hyperfocus towards these areas, you transform what many perceive as a limitation into a potent professional asset.

The first step in leveraging hyperfocus effectively is selecting the right projects. Opt for tasks that inherently pique your interest or challenge you in a way that keeps your brain engaged. Projects that involve problem-solving, creative thinking, or a degree of complexity often provide the mental stimulation needed to trigger hyperfocus. For instance, if you're in a technical field, you might choose to work on developing a new software feature that requires deep coding skills, or if you're in the arts, a detailed graphic design project might be just the right fit. These tasks are not just about keeping you busy; they're about engaging your mind in a way that hyperfocus thrives on. By aligning your projects with your natural inclinations and abilities, you not only increase your productivity but also enhance your job satisfaction, as you're more likely to enjoy working on tasks that interest you.

Balancing hyperfocus with teamwork and collaboration presents its own set of challenges and opportunities. While hyperfocus can make you an incredible asset in solo projects, professional environments often require collaboration. To ensure your hyperfocus becomes a team asset, communicate openly with your colleagues about your working style. Plan your tasks so that your periods of hyperfocus align with project phases where deep work is most beneficial, such as the initial research phase or the final completion stage. During collaborative phases, you might need to adjust your focus to allow for team interaction and input. Tools like shared project management software can help you keep track of both individual and team tasks, ensuring that your periods of hyperfocus do not overshadow collaborative responsibilities. Additionally, by educating your team about how ADHD affects your work style, you foster a better understanding and can develop strategies together that leverage your strengths for the benefit of the entire team.

Managing hyperfocus to prevent burnout is crucial. Intense concentration can lead to mental fatigue if not properly managed. It's important to recognize the signs of burnout, which can include feeling mentally exhausted, irritable, or less motivated. To mitigate these risks, set clear boundaries for how long you spend on tasks. Use timers to remind yourself to take breaks, ideally before you feel fatigued. During these breaks, engage in activities that help you recharge, such as a short walk, meditation, or a casual chat with a colleague. These pauses are not just downtime; they are vital intervals that allow your brain to rest and reset, enhancing your productivity and creativity when you return to work. Additionally, ensure that your workday has a hard stop time to prevent work from bleeding into your personal time, which is essential for maintaining a healthy work-life balance.

By embracing these strategies, you can effectively transform your hyperfocus from a wildcard into a well-played ace in your professional repertoire. This approach not only enhances your work performance but also contributes to a more fulfilling and balanced professional life, where ADHD traits are not just managed but celebrated as part of your unique professional identity.

Advocating for Accommodations and Understanding at Work

Navigating the workplace with ADHD can often feel like trying to fit a square peg into a round hole, especially if the work environment isn't attuned to neurodiverse needs. Understanding your legal rights regarding accommodations is crucial. In many regions, laws such as the Americans with Disabilities Act (ADA) in the U.S., mandate that employers provide reasonable accommodations for employees with disabilities, including those with ADHD, as long as it doesn't impose undue hardship on the business. These accommodations are designed to level the playing field, providing you with the tools needed to perform your job duties effectively. It's important to familiarize yourself with these rights and the specific procedures for requesting accommodations in your workplace. Often, this will involve providing a formal diagnosis and possibly a detailed request explaining how the accommodations will aid in your job performance.

Communicating your needs effectively is paramount in advocating for accommodations. It starts with a candid yet professional conversation with your employer about your ADHD and how it affects your work. Be clear and specific about what accommodations you need, such as a flexible schedule, a quieter workspace, or the ability to work from home periodically. It's helpful to explain how these accommodations will not only benefit you but can enhance your productivity and quality of work, aligning your interests with those of your employer. For instance, the option to work remotely on days when you need hyper-focus can drastically increase your output and decrease potential distractions. Prepare for this discussion by outlining your points in advance, perhaps even rehearsing them. This preparation can help you present your case clearly and confidently, increasing the likelihood of a favorable outcome.

Implementing ADHD-friendly work practices can transform your work experience and output. Practical examples include structured daily check-ins to help prioritize tasks, using noise-canceling headphones to minimize auditory distractions, or access to project management software that helps keep you organized. Another effective accommodation is the modification of work hours or break times to align with your productivity patterns—perhaps shorter, more frequent breaks or the flexibility to start later in the day when you're more alert. Employers can also provide written instructions and feedback instead of verbal, which can be easier for someone with ADHD to process and refer back to. These adjustments help create a work environment where you can utilize your strengths more effectively.

Fostering an inclusive work environment goes beyond personal accommodations. It involves advocating for policies and practices that benefit all employees, including those with ADHD. This could mean proposing regular training sessions on neurodiversity, creating an employee resource group for neurodivergent employees, or establishing more transparent communication protocols that benefit everyone. By championing these initiatives, you not only improve your own work conditions but also contribute to a culture of inclusivity and understanding. This proactive approach not only positions you as a leader in workplace diversity but also helps break down the stigmas often associated with ADHD, paving the way for future employees who might be struggling in silence.

Advocating for workplace accommodations requires a blend of self-awareness, legal knowledge, clear communication, and strategic action. By understanding your rights, effectively communicating your needs, implementing practical accommodations, and fostering an inclusive environment, you create a more supportive and productive workplace. This not only enhances your work life but also sets a precedent for openness, diversity, and accommodation that can enrich your entire organization.

As we wrap up this exploration into workplace accommodations and advocacy, we've equipped you with the tools and insights needed to transform challenges into opportunities, both for personal growth and broader organizational advancement. The strategies discussed here are part of a larger narrative of embracing and leveraging ADHD in all areas of life, affirming that with the right support and understanding, individuals with ADHD can not only succeed but excel. Moving forward, the next chapter will build on these foundations, focusing on cultivating lasting relationships and building a supportive community.

CHAPTER 10: BUILDING A SUPPORTIVE COMMUNITY

Imagine stepping into a room where everyone understands the whirlwind of thoughts that often flood your mind, where the challenges that sometimes leave you feeling isolated are the very threads that connect you to others. This chapter dives into the transformative world of ADHD support groups, where shared experiences and collective wisdom pave the way for personal growth and empowerment. Here, you're not alone; you're part of a community that gets it, a community that supports each other through the ups and downs of navigating life with ADHD.

Finding and Engaging with ADHD Support Groups

Benefits of Support Groups

Joining an ADHD support group can feel like finding a beacon in a stormy sea. These groups offer a spectrum of benefits that extend far beyond simple companionship. Shared experiences, for instance, are at the heart of what makes these groups so invaluable. They provide reassurance that you're not alone in your struggles, offering a sense of belonging that can be hard to find elsewhere. The advice you'll receive comes from lived experiences, resonating more deeply and practically than generic guidelines often found in books or articles. Emotional support, too, is readily available, as members often provide encouragement and understanding in a judgment-free environment. This emotional solidarity can be a powerful antidote to the isolation and misunderstanding that ADHD can sometimes bring into your life.

Finding the Right Group

The journey to finding the right ADHD support group might require some navigation, but the destination is well worth the effort. Start by considering what format suits you best—whether it's face-to-face meetings that offer the warmth of human connection or online forums that provide convenience and a broad reach. Local mental health organizations, hospitals, or even a simple internet search can point you in the direction of these groups. Websites such as CHADD (Children and Adults with Attention-Deficit/Hyperactivity Disorder) offer resources for locating support groups in your area. When choosing a group, consider the meeting structure and the group's focus—some might center around discussion, while others may offer educational resources or guest speakers. Ensure that the group's atmosphere aligns with your needs: a place where confidentiality is respected and where you feel safe and supported.

Engaging Effectively

Active participation is the key to making the most out of ADHD support groups. Engaging effectively means more than just attending meetings; it involves sharing your experiences, listening actively to others, and applying what you learn. Encourage a two-way exchange of information and support. Be open about your challenges and achievements, ask questions, and offer your insights when others share their experiences. This active engagement helps you gain more comprehensive insights into managing ADHD and fosters a stronger connection with group members, enhancing the sense of community.

Starting Your Own Group

If your search doesn't lead you to the right group, or if you aspire to tailor a community that specifically addresses certain aspects of ADHD, consider starting your own support group. This initiative can be incredibly rewarding, not just for you but for others who are seeking support. Begin by defining the group's purpose and structure—decide what focus the group will have, how often it will meet, and where meetings will be held. Reach out to local mental health professionals who might offer guidance or support. Promote your group through social media, local community boards, and by partnering with local mental health organizations. As your group grows, foster a welcoming and supportive environment that encourages openness and mutual support. Remember, the goal is to create a space where individuals feel valued and understood, a community where every member can both teach and learn, share and grow.

Steps to Start Your Own ADHD Support Group:

1. Define Your Vision: Identify the focus and goals of your group.

2. Find a Venue: Choose a convenient and accessible location for meetings.

3. Seek Guidance: Contact local mental health professionals for support.

4. Promote Your Group: Use social media, local community boards, and partnerships to spread the word.

5. Foster Engagement: Create a welcoming environment that encourages active participation and mutual support.

Online Resources and Communities for Men with ADHD

Navigating the vast landscape of the internet can often feel like trying to find a trail in a dense forest. For adults with ADHD, the online world offers a rich repository of communities and resources that can provide support, education, and connection. Understanding how to effectively find and participate in these online spaces can transform them from overwhelming to invaluable. Online forums, social media groups, and blogs dedicated to ADHD are more than just informational resources; they are vibrant communities where you can share experiences, learn from others, and even find solace in the stories of those who traverse similar paths.

When you begin exploring online ADHD communities, start with well-established platforms like ADDitude Magazine's forums or the ADHD subreddit, which host a wide array of discussions ranging from coping strategies to personal success stories. Social media platforms like Facebook and Twitter also boast numerous ADHD-focused groups and pages that offer daily tips and community support. Engaging in these spaces requires a bit of strategy to gain the most benefit. Prioritize joining groups that are active, where posts are frequent and discussions are ongoing. Look for communities that have clear guidelines and moderators to ensure discussions remain respectful and constructive. Once you join, don't hesitate to introduce yourself and share your journey. Engaging isn't just about seeking answers; it's also about sharing your insights, which can be incredibly validating and helpful to others.

Leveraging online resources effectively can greatly enhance your understanding and management of ADHD. Beyond community forums and social media groups, numerous websites offer valuable educational materials and tools specifically designed for adults with ADHD. Websites like CHADD (Children and Adults with Attention-Deficit/Hyperactivity Disorder) provide comprehensive articles, webinars, and toolkits that cover everything from the latest research in ADHD management to practical tips for everyday living. Podcasts such as "Distraction" and "ADHD reWired" offer insights and advice through a more personal and relatable medium, allowing you to gain knowledge and support while on the go. Engaging with these resources can be particularly useful; many sites offer interactive elements like quizzes or self-assessments that can help you better understand your particular manifestation of ADHD or track your progress over time.

Privacy and safety online are paramount, especially when discussing personal health information such as your ADHD diagnosis. When participating in forums and social media groups, be cautious about how much personal information you share. Customize your privacy settings to control who can see your posts and comments. Be wary of advice that seems unconventional or that encourages going against professional medical advice. Always cross-reference information with reliable sources or consult with a healthcare professional before making changes to your management plans. Remember, the goal of engaging in these communities and resources is to enhance your understanding and management of ADHD, not to replace professional advice.

Contributing to online ADHD communities can be incredibly rewarding. By sharing your own experiences and insights, you not only enrich the conversation but also contribute to a larger body of knowledge that can help others feel less alone in their struggles. Write about your successes and setbacks, share tips that have worked for you, or provide encouragement to those who might be struggling. Your voice is a vital part of the ADHD community online; your unique perspective can provide hope and help to those who may be seeking support and understanding. By actively contributing, you strengthen the community and foster a space of mutual support and growth, which is essential for all individuals navigating life with ADHD.

Creating Your ADHD Support Network

Building a robust support network is much like assembling a personalized toolkit; each tool serves a specific purpose, helping you navigate various aspects of life with ADHD. Identifying supportive individuals who either understand ADHD or are open to learning about it is your starting point. These individuals could be friends who notice when you're overwhelmed and step in without needing to be asked, family members who encourage rather than criticize, or colleagues who share strategies for managing similar challenges. The key is to look for those who display empathy, patience, and a willingness to support you in practical ways. This might mean having someone who will check in with you regularly, a friend who can help you brainstorm solutions to organizational challenges, or a family member who ensures you feel heard and valued rather than judged.

As you identify these individuals, consider the diversity of your network, which should ideally include not only personal connections but also professionals and peers with ADHD. Such diversity ensures a well-rounded support system that can offer a range of perspectives and solutions. Professionals, such as therapists or coaches, bring a wealth of knowledge and strategies tailored to managing ADHD. Their expertise can help you navigate the more complex aspects of ADHD, providing guidance that's grounded in the latest research and practices. Peers with ADHD offer the camaraderie of shared experiences. They can provide insights and strategies that have worked for them in a relatable way that professionals might not. And don't overlook the value of non-ADHD allies; these are individuals who, although they might not share your specific experiences, bring empathy, support, and a different perspective that can be equally valuable.

Understanding the roles within your support network is crucial. You might think of these roles in terms of a sports team, where each player has a specific position and set of responsibilities contributing to the team's overall success. Some might serve as mentors, offering guidance based on their own experiences and successes. Others might be accountability partners who help you stay on track with your goals, providing gentle reminders or encouragement to keep you moving forward. Emotional support contacts are those you can turn to when you need to talk, offering a listening ear and reassurance when you're facing tough days. Each role is distinct but equally important, ensuring you have the right support at the right time.

Nurturing these relationships is as important as forming them. This means investing time and effort into maintaining and strengthening these connections. Regular check-ins, whether through calls, texts, or meet-ups, help keep these relationships vibrant and ensure that your network remains supportive. Be proactive in expressing gratitude and appreciation for their support, which not only reinforces your bonds but also makes your supporters feel valued. It's also important to reciprocate wherever possible. Support networks are at their best when all members feel supported, so look for opportunities to give back to those who have aided you. This might mean sharing your own experiences and strategies, offering to listen when others need to talk, or simply being there for them as they have been for you.

In building and nurturing your ADHD support network, remember that the quality of connections often outweighs the quantity. A few strong, reliable relationships can be more beneficial than numerous superficial ones. This network, built on understanding, diversity, and mutual support, becomes a powerful resource in managing ADHD, providing you with a solid foundation from which to face both challenges and successes.

The Role of Therapy and Coaching in ADHD Management

Navigating ADHD can sometimes feel like trying to decipher an intricate map without a compass. This is where professional support in the form of therapy and coaching can become invaluable. Therapists and coaches who specialize in ADHD are akin to navigators who help chart a course through the often-turbulent waters of managing symptoms and enhancing personal growth. The benefits of such professional guidance are manifold. Primarily, these professionals provide personalized strategies that are tailored to your specific ADHD challenges and strengths, which can significantly improve your daily functioning and overall quality of life. For instance, a therapist might help you develop coping strategies for anxiety that stems from ADHD-related challenges, while a coach might focus on practical techniques to enhance your time management or organizational skills.

Finding the right professional is crucial and can feel daunting at first. It's important to look for a therapist or coach who not only specializes in ADHD but also aligns with your personality and therapeutic needs. Start by seeking recommendations from local ADHD support groups or trusted healthcare providers. When researching potential therapists or coaches, review their qualifications and any reviews or testimonials from other clients with ADHD. It's often helpful to schedule an initial consultation to see if their approach resonates with your expectations and needs. During this meeting, discuss their understanding of ADHD, their experience with similar cases, and their approach to treatment or coaching. This conversation can provide significant insights into whether they could be the right fit for you.

Integrating the insights and strategies from therapy or coaching into your daily life is where the real transformation begins. This integration involves taking the tools and techniques learned during sessions and applying them to everyday situations. For instance, if your coach has worked with you on a strategy for managing interruptions at work that derail your focus, start implementing this strategy consistently to see how it affects your productivity and stress levels. Similarly, if your therapist has helped you develop techniques for managing stress or emotional dysregulation, use these techniques daily to help stabilize your mood and improve your interactions with others. Consistency is key—the more you practice these strategies, the more ingrained they will become in your routine, enhancing their effectiveness.

Group therapy sessions and workshops can also be incredibly beneficial, especially for those who find strength in shared experiences.

These settings offer a unique dynamic where you can learn not only from the facilitator but also from the experiences and insights of other participants. The collective wisdom of a group can provide multiple perspectives on common challenges, opening up new strategies or solutions that might not have been considered in one-on-one sessions. Moreover, group settings can reinforce that you are not alone in your struggles, which is often a powerful realization that can diminish feelings of isolation or frustration. Workshops designed specifically for individuals with ADHD can focus on particular skills, such as organizational techniques or social skills, providing practical training that can be immediately applied to daily life.

Educating Friends and Family about ADHD

Understanding ADHD is not just a personal journey; it involves those around you—your friends and family. Educating them about what ADHD really entails plays a crucial role in fostering a supportive environment. This isn't about seeking sympathy but about cultivating an informed support system that truly understands the highs and lows of ADHD. When friends and family get why you might forget details, why you might interrupt during conversations, or why you sometimes seem disorganized, their responses are more likely to be supportive rather than critical.

Initiating conversations about ADHD can sometimes feel daunting. It's essential to approach these discussions with clarity and simplicity. Begin by explaining what ADHD is not—it's not a lack of intelligence or an inability to focus all the time. ADHD involves challenges with regulating attention—too much sometimes, too little at others. Use analogies if it helps; for example, likening the ADHD mind to a browser with too many tabs open can be a relatable way to explain how your mind works. Address common misconceptions directly. For instance, ADHD isn't just about being hyperactive or distracted; it's a complex neurodevelopmental disorder that affects various aspects of life and functioning. These discussions should aim to replace misjudgments with empathy, paving the way for deeper understanding and better relational dynamics.

For those who want to dive deeper, provide resources that offer more comprehensive insights into ADHD. Recommend books like "Driven to Distraction" by Edward Hallowell and John Ratey, which is a seminal work in understanding ADHD across different stages of life. Websites such as ADDitude Magazine offer a treasure trove of articles about daily living with ADHD, coping strategies, and personal stories. Encourage them to explore documentaries or YouTube channels dedicated to ADHD that provide both scientific information and personal experiences. These resources can be invaluable for friends and family, giving them a well-rounded understanding of ADHD beyond your personal experiences.

Setting boundaries and managing expectations is another vital aspect of these educational efforts. It's about communicating what you need—whether it's time to decompress after a busy day or the need for reminders in a non-nagging way. Explain how unpredictability in your attention and energy levels might affect plans and commitments and discuss ways to handle such situations together. For instance, having a code word or signal that means you're feeling overwhelmed can be a discreet way to communicate your needs in social settings. It's also helpful to set clear expectations about what kind of support you find helpful. Whether it's helping to keep track of time during tasks or just listening when you need to talk about a tough day, specifying these can prevent frustration on both sides and make your support system more effective.

Through these efforts, the aim is not just to educate but to empower those around you to be proactive supporters in your journey with ADHD, rather than passive bystanders. This not only enhances your relationships but also contributes to a broader understanding of ADHD, reducing stigma and fostering a more inclusive environment.

As this chapter closes, reflect on the power of community and communication in managing ADHD. The strategies discussed here are not just about coping; they're about thriving through active engagement, informed support, and mutual understanding. Up next, we'll explore some biohacking techniques and creative solutions.

CHAPTER 11:
UNCONVENTIONAL WISDOM AND CREATIVE SOLUTIONS

Imagine standing at the edge of innovation, where traditional approaches to managing ADHD blend with cutting-edge techniques that offer new hope and possibilities. This chapter delves into the realm of biohacking—a space where science meets self-experimentation, creating opportunities to fine-tune your body and mind in ways that uniquely suit your ADHD.

Biohacking for ADHD: Supplements and Neurofeedback

Supplements That Target ADHD Symptoms

Diving into the world of biohacking, we first explore the role of supplements in managing ADHD symptoms. As we've discussed previously, essential fatty acids like Omega-3s, minerals such as zinc and magnesium, are more than just nutritional supplements; they are potential game-changers in the management of ADHD. Scientific research suggests that Omega-3 fatty acids, found abundantly in fish oils, play a crucial role in brain function and development. They are believed to enhance the cognitive functions impaired by ADHD, such as memory and focus. Zinc contributes to neurotransmitter function and is thought to help regulate the impulsive behavior associated with ADHD. Magnesium, often called the relaxation mineral, helps in calming the nervous system, which can be particularly beneficial for those with ADHD experiencing hyperactivity and sleep difficulties.

Integrating these supplements into your daily regimen could potentially amplify your brain's ability to manage the symptoms of ADHD. However, it's crucial to approach supplementation under medical guidance to tailor the dosage to your specific needs and avoid any potential interactions with medications.

Introduction to Neurofeedback

Neurofeedback therapy represents a frontier in ADHD management, providing a real-time look into brainwave patterns. This non-invasive technique uses EEG sensors to monitor brain activity and feed that information back to you via visual or auditory signals. By training to modify these brainwaves, you can potentially enhance your brain's ability to concentrate and relax, thereby reducing the core symptoms of ADHD. For instance, training your brain to increase beta waves can improve focus and reduce impulsivity, while enhancing alpha waves can help in managing anxiety and improving relaxation.

Neurofeedback is a promising tool for those seeking to gain a deeper understanding of their neurological functioning and take an active role in modulating their brain's activity. It offers a personalized approach as each session is tailored to the individual's unique brain patterns, making it a highly targeted method to potentially alleviate the symptoms of ADHD.

Personal Experiences with Biohacking

The journey of biohacking is personal and varied. Many individuals with ADHD have turned to biohacking as a means to reclaim control over their symptoms and enhance their quality of life. Anecdotal evidence from these personal journeys often highlights profound impacts. For instance, some report significant reductions in impulsivity and improvements in focus after consistent supplementation with Omega-3s or after a series of neurofeedback sessions. These stories provide not only hope but also practical frameworks that you might consider exploring in your own life.

Safety and Efficacy Considerations

While the potential of biohacking in managing ADHD is immense, it's crucial to navigate this field with caution. The efficacy of such interventions can vary widely among individuals, and what works for one person might not work for another. It is essential to consult with healthcare professionals to understand the potential benefits and risks. For supplements, this means ensuring that the dosages are safe and that they do not interfere with other medications. For neurofeedback, it involves selecting qualified practitioners who can guide you safely through the process.

The Role of Creative Expression in Managing ADHD

Creative activities, spanning from painting and writing to playing music, are not just hobbies; for individuals with ADHD, they embody potent therapeutic tools. The act of creating engages the brain in unique ways that can alleviate many of the common symptoms associated with ADHD. For instance, engaging in a drawing session or crafting a piece of music provides a structured outlet for the excess energy and impulsivity often experienced. These activities demand focused attention but in a dynamic and enjoyable way, which can be far more appealing than static tasks. The rhythmic strokes of a brush or the structured patterns of music notes can serve as a meditative practice, helping to calm the mind and reduce feelings of anxiety or restlessness.

Moreover, creative expression offers a legitimate outlet for hyperfocus, a common trait in many individuals with ADHD. Hyperfocus can be a double-edged sword; while it can lead to significant productivity in tasks that catch one's interest, it can also lead to neglect of other necessary tasks. Channeling this intense concentration into creative projects can yield profound satisfaction and significant achievements in art, writing, or other expressive activities. This focused engagement also helps to cultivate a deeper level of patience and persistence, qualities that might not come as naturally in other areas of life for those with ADHD. Additionally, the completed creative product provides tangible evidence of achievement, which can boost self-esteem and improve mood.

The impact of creative outlets on individuals with ADHD is not just anecdotal; several case studies highlight the transformative effects of arts on personal and professional lives. Consider the story of a graphic designer who struggled with traditional organizational tasks at work but found immense success and fulfillment in complex design projects that others found too daunting. His ability to hyperfocus allowed him to excel in creating intricate designs, eventually leading him to start his own successful design firm. Another inspiring example is a writer with ADHD who used her narrative skills to craft compelling stories, despite struggling with concentration when it came to everyday tasks. Her books, often filled with dynamic, fast-paced plots, have not only been bestsellers but have also provided her a therapeutic outlet for her restless energy and imagination.

For those eager to start exploring their creative sides, finding the right medium is crucial. Start by identifying activities that naturally intrigue you. If you're visually oriented, painting or drawing might be a good fit. If you love stories, try writing short stories or poetry. For those who are musically inclined, learning an instrument could be a fulfilling endeavor. Begin small; you don't need to commit to large projects right away. Experiment with different forms of creative expression to find what truly captivates your interest and suits your lifestyle. Incorporating these activities into your daily routine can be as simple as scheduling short, regular sessions where you can sketch, write, or play music. Over time, these creative sessions can become a cherished part of your day, offering both a respite and a productive challenge.

The journey of integrating creativity into your life with ADHD is not just about managing symptoms but also about rediscovering joy and passion in activities that resonate with your unique mind. Whether it's through painting landscapes, writing poems, or composing music, each creative endeavor provides a valuable channel for expression and emotional equilibrium, proving that within the challenges of ADHD lies the potential for remarkable creativity and achievement.

Adventure and Risk-Taking: Channeling ADHD Energy Positively

Exploring the positive aspects of risk-taking in individuals with ADHD reveals a dynamic interplay between innate impulsivity and the potential for extraordinary creativity and problem-solving. Often, the spontaneous decisions and willingness to leap into new experiences can lead to innovative solutions and creative breakthroughs not immediately obvious to the more cautious mind. For many with ADHD, this propensity for risk-taking is not merely about seeking thrills; it's a fundamental part of how they interact with the world, generating novel ideas and approaches that stand out in their unpredictability and ingenuity. This inclination towards innovative thinking makes individuals with ADHD valuable in roles and environments where out-of-the-box thinking is not just appreciated but essential.

The allure of adventure sports for those with ADHD can be particularly strong, offering an intense, immersive experience that aligns well with the ADHD need for high stimulation. Activities like rock climbing, mountain biking, and surfing do more than just provide physical outlets for pent-up energy. They require a level of focus and present-moment awareness that can be therapeutic for the ADHD mind, which often juggles multiple thoughts and stimuli. The immediate feedback from engaging in these sports—such as the rush of successfully navigating a tricky trail or catching a perfect wave—provides a direct, tangible reward for sustained attention and effort, reinforcing these behaviors. Moreover, the structured yet unpredictable nature of these activities provides a unique way to experience excitement and challenge without the negative repercussions that unstructured risk-taking might entail.

However, balancing the natural inclination towards risk-taking with the need for safety and responsibility is crucial. It's important to approach adventure sports and other high-energy activities with a strategy that acknowledges the thrill but safeguards against potential harm. This involves choosing activities that match one's physical abilities and emotional readiness. For instance, if new to mountain biking, starting on moderate trails and gradually increasing difficulty can provide the stimulation needed without undue risk. Additionally, using proper safety gear, like helmets and harnesses, and adhering to safety protocols cannot be overstated. It's also beneficial to engage in these activities under the guidance of professionals or experienced peers who can provide instructions and support, ensuring that the adventure remains within safe boundaries.

For those looking to channel their ADHD-driven energy into safe yet adventurous activities, several options can be tailored to individual preferences and abilities. Archery, for example, combines the thrill of hitting a target with the discipline of steady, controlled movements, offering a balance of excitement and focus. Geocaching, a real-world treasure hunt using GPS, provides an adventurous quest that also stimulates the mind through problem-solving and navigation challenges. For the more physically inclined, obstacle course races like Spartan Race or Tough Mudder provide a challenging and exhilarating environment that tests physical and mental endurance, with the safety of structured competition. These activities not only cater to the adventurous spirit but also foster skills like focus, persistence, and strategic planning, which are beneficial beyond the scope of the activity itself.

Engaging in these activities provides an outlet for the adventurous impulses and high energy typical of many individuals with ADHD, allowing for a healthy expression of these traits. By focusing on activities that combine excitement with structure and safety, you can enjoy the positive aspects of risk-taking without its potential pitfalls, leading to a more balanced and fulfilling experience.

Future Trends in ADHD Treatment and Understanding

The landscape of ADHD treatment and understanding is ever-evolving, with new research and technologies continuously emerging that promise to reshape our approach to this complex condition. One of the most exciting developments is the advent of personalized medicine in the field of ADHD, driven by deeper genetic and neurobiological insights. Researchers are now beginning to identify specific genetic markers that may not only help in diagnosing ADHD more accurately but also in tailoring treatments to individual genetic profiles. This precision approach could revolutionize treatment plans, making them more effective by aligning them closely with the unique neurochemical makeup of each individual.

Furthermore, the integration of technology in managing ADHD is seeing unprecedented growth. Wearable tech, for instance, is being explored for its potential to monitor physiological indicators like heart rate and skin conductance, which can offer real-time insights into an individual's stress and anxiety levels—common challenges for those with ADHD. This data can be used to alert the wearer to potential overstimulation before it becomes overwhelming, allowing them to take proactive steps to manage their state. Apps that use cognitive behavioral therapy (CBT) techniques are also becoming increasingly sophisticated, providing users with accessible, on-the-go tools for managing symptoms. Future innovations might include augmented reality experiences that can help individuals with ADHD improve their social skills or manage sensory overload in controlled, immersive environments.

The evolution of ADHD diagnosis is also noteworthy, with diagnostic criteria becoming more nuanced. Traditional methods often relied heavily on subjective assessments, which could lead to inconsistencies and misdiagnosis. Now, advancements in neuroimaging and other diagnostic technologies are being combined with traditional approaches to offer a more comprehensive view of an individual's neurological functioning. This not only aids in more accurate diagnoses but also helps in understanding the broad spectrum of ADHD presentations. It acknowledges that ADHD does not look the same in everyone, paving the way for more customized treatment approaches that address the specific manifestations of ADHD in each individual.

ADHD's placement within the broader context of mental health is also undergoing a significant shift. There is a growing recognition of the need for a holistic approach that considers not just the neurological aspects but also the emotional and psychological impacts of ADHD. Mental health professionals are increasingly advocating for integrated treatment plans that address comorbid conditions such as anxiety and depression, which frequently accompany ADHD. This holistic approach emphasizes the importance of a supportive community and the development of coping strategies that enhance overall well-being, not just the management of ADHD symptoms.

The exploration of these future trends not only highlights the dynamic nature of ADHD research and treatment but also offers hope and excitement about the possibilities for more effective management and understanding of ADHD. The ongoing advancements in genetics, technology, diagnostic criteria, and holistic care are crafting a future where individuals with ADHD have access to highly personalized, effective, and comprehensive treatment plans that support their needs in all dimensions of health.

As we close this chapter on the future trends in ADHD treatment and understanding, we look forward to a landscape rich with promise and innovation. The journey ahead is one of continued exploration and adaptation, as we aim to transform the challenges of today into the victories of tomorrow.

Keeping the game alive

Now you have everything you need to improve focus, increase productivity, manage your symptoms, and thrive in life, it's time to pass on your newfound knowledge and show other readers where they can find the same help.

Simply by leaving your honest opinion of this book on Amazon, you'll show other men with adult ADHD where they can find the information they're looking for, and pass their passion for managing ADHD forward.

Thank you for your help. The journey to managing ADHD is kept alive when we pass on our knowledge – and you're helping us to do just that.

Click the link below to leave your review on Amazon.

Your feedback not only helps others find this valuable resource, but it also keeps the spirit of learning and growth alive within our community. By sharing your experience, you're making a difference in the lives of men who, like you, are striving to thrive with ADHD.

Thank you from the bottom of my heart.

Your biggest fan, Mark Fitzgerald

Conclusion

Reflecting on our journey together through the pages of this book, we've navigated the complex world of adult ADHD in men with a focus not just on understanding but on action. From unpacking the neurological foundations of ADHD to exploring practical strategies for managing daily challenges, we've embarked on a path of empowerment and self-discovery. Together, we've learned to view ADHD not just as a series of challenges to overcome, but as a unique part of your identity that can be harnessed for personal and professional triumph.

Key Takeaways:

- The importance of understanding the neurological underpinnings of ADHD and how they affect behavior and cognition.

- Practical strategies for managing time, emotions, relationships, and workplace challenges.

- The power of lifestyle adjustments, including diet, exercise, and routine, to enhance focus and reduce impulsivity.

- Techniques for leveraging the strengths of ADHD to enhance creativity, problem-solving skills, and adaptability.

As we close this chapter of your journey, remember that this book is not an endpoint but a stepping stone. Managing ADHD is a dynamic, lifelong process. The strategies and insights we've discussed are tools in your toolkit, adaptable as your life evolves. Stay curious and open to growth, and be willing to adjust your approaches as you learn more about yourself and your needs.

I encourage you to take proactive steps every day. Use the strategies that resonate with you, reach out for professional guidance when needed, and continue to educate yourself about ADHD. Set small, achievable goals that will lead you toward the larger vision you have for your life.

You are not alone on this journey. The strength of community in navigating ADHD cannot be overstressed. Whether it's friends who understand, supportive family members, engaging support groups, or knowledgeable professionals, building a network of support is crucial. They are your allies, ready to offer a helping hand or an understanding ear when you need it most.

Despite the hurdles ADHD might present, it is entirely possible to lead a fulfilling, productive, and successful life. Embrace your ADHD with confidence and optimism. Let it be a source of unique strength and creativity in your life. There is immense power in owning your story and using it to shape a future that aligns with your aspirations.

As we part ways through these pages, my hope for you remains steadfast. I believe in your potential to navigate the challenges and harness the strengths of your ADHD. Your journey is uniquely yours, filled with opportunities to carve out success on your own terms.

Here's to embracing your uniqueness, continuing to grow, and stepping confidently into a future filled with promise.

Thank you for allowing me to be a part of your journey. Here's to
moving forward with courage, support, and a heart full of hope.

References

- *The neurobiological basis of ADHD - PMC* https://www.ncbi.nlm.nih.gov/pmc/articles/PMC3016271/

- *How to Improve Executive Function Skills in ADHD Adults ...* https://www.additudemag.com/how-to-improve-executive-function-adhd/

- *Understanding Hyperfocus and ADHD* https://health.clevelandclinic.org/hyperfocus-and-adhd

- *Rejection Sensitive Dysphoria (RSD): Symptoms & Treatment* https://my.clevelandclinic.org/health/diseases/24099-rejection-sensitive-dysphoria-rsd

- *Unlocking The Power Of Neurodiversity: Embracing ADHD Awareness Month* https://www.forbes.com/sites/onemind/2023/11/06/unlocking-the-power-of-neurodiversity-embracing-adhd-awareness-month/

- *Challenging The Stigma: ADHD In Society And The Workplace* https://nuvistamentalhealth.com/2024/03/28/challenging-the-stigma-adhd-in-society-and-the-workplace/

- *ADHD Personal Stories: Real-Life Success ... - ADDitude* https://www.additudemag.com/adhd-personal-stories-real-life-people-living-with-adhd/

- *How to Practice Self Compassion with ADHD* https://www.additudemag.com/self-compassion-practice-adhd-shame/

- *ADHD-Friendly Workspace Design for Better Focus* https://adhdneuro.com/blog/adhd-friendly-workspace-design-for-better-focus

- *How the Pomodoro Technique Can Help With ADHD ...* https://www.choosingtherapy.com/pomodoro-technique-adhd/

- *Best Productivity Apps for Adults with ADHD: Our Top Picks* https://www.additudemag.com/best-productivity-apps-adhd-adults/

- *A Potential Natural Treatment for Attention-Deficit ...* https://www.ncbi.nlm.nih.gov/pmc/articles/PMC1448497/

- *Adult ADHD and Relationships* https://www.helpguide.org/articles/add-adhd/adult-adhd-attention-deficit-disorder-and-relationships.htm

- *Improve Listening Skills with Adult ADHD* https://www.additudemag.com/listening-skills-better-listener-adult-adhd-tips/

- *ADHD and Emotional Dysregulation: Signs & How To Improve* https://www.beyondbooksmart.com/executive-functioning-strategies-blog/adhd-emotional-dysregulation

- *ADHD and Boundaries: The 4 C's of Boundary Setting* https://www.unconventionalorganisation.com/post/adhd-and-boundaries-the-4-c-s-of-boundary-setting

- *Budgeting Tips That Work for ADHD Brains* https://www.additudemag.com/budgeting-tips-for-adhd-brains/

- *Impulse Buying and ADHD: 12 Tips to Shop Smart, Spend ...* https://www.additudemag.com/impulse-buying-money-problems-adhd-adults/

- *Managing Money and ADHD: Expenses and Goals* https://chadd.org/for-adults/managing-money-and-adhd-expenses-and-goals/

- *Managing Money and ADHD: Minding Your Debts* https://chadd.org/for-adults/managing-money-and-adhd-minding-your-debts/

- *How to Practice Mindfulness with ADHD: Meditation for Adults* https://www.additudemag.com/how-to-practice-mindfulness-adhd/

- *Effectiveness of cognitive behavioural-based interventions for ...* https://bpspsychub.onlinelibrary.wiley.com/doi/abs/10.1111/papt.12455

- *Physical exercise in attention deficit hyperactivity disorder* https://www.ncbi.nlm.nih.gov/pmc/articles/PMC6945516/

- *Navigating Stress and ADHD: Tips to Reduce Triggers and ...* https://add.org/stress-and-adhd/

- *Tips to Organize Your Home With ADHD - WebMD* https://www.webmd.com/add-adhd/tips-organize-home-adhd

- *Navigating ADHD As a Project Manager* https://leantime.io/navigating-adhd-as-a-project-manager/

- *How to Set Goals and Achieve Them with ADHD - ADDitude* https://www.additudemag.com/how-to-set-goals-achieve-them-adhd/

- *The Ultimate Digital Decluttering Strategy* https://www.usemotion.com/blog/digital-declutter

- *ADHD Diet For Adults: Foods to Eat and Avoid - ADDA* https://add.org/adhd-diet/

- *undefined* undefined

- *Physical exercise in attention deficit hyperactivity disorder* https://www.ncbi.nlm.nih.gov/pmc/articles/PMC6945516/

- *9 Tips for Creating a Routine for Adults with ADHD* https://psychcentral.com/adhd/9-tips-for-creating-a-routine-for-adults-with-adhd

- *Top 5 Potential Benefits of ADHD for Employees - ADDA* https://add.org/benefits-of-adhd-employees/

- *8 Ways Employers Can Make the Workplace More ADHD Friendly* https://blog.jobbio.com/2018/09/03/make-the-workplace-more-adhd-friendly/

- *ADHD isn't a career killer. Just ask these executives* https://www.cnn.com/2019/07/02/success/executives-with-adhd/index.html

- *ADHD Accommodations at Work: Your Rights to Disability ...* https://www.additudemag.com/adhd-law-americans-with-disabilities-act/

- *ADHD support groups: Benefits, options, and more* https://www.medicalnewstoday.com/articles/adhd-support-groups

- *ADDA Support Group Manual* https://add.org/wp-content/uploads/2015/04/ADHD_Group_Instruction_Manual.pdf

- *Peer Support for Men with ADHD - ADDA* https://add.org/men-becoming-best-peer-group-men-adhd/

- *Cognitive Behavioral Therapy vs. ADHD Coaching* https://www.additudemag.com/adhd-therapy-cbt-vs-coaching/

- *undefined* undefined

- *Experiences of neurofeedback therapists in treating ...* https://www.ncbi.nlm.nih.gov/pmc/articles/PMC9350471/

- *Creativity and ADHD: Don't Stifle Your Creative Mind* https://www.additudemag.com/adhd-creativity-brain-health/

- *Emerging drugs for the treatment of attention-deficit ... - PubMed* https://pubmed.ncbi.nlm.nih.gov/32938246/#:~:text=Stand%2Dalone%20emerging%20treatments%20for,to%20sup port%20market%20access%20requests.